Antonio Alfani

Tales the Table from

Dear Clay Family,
Buon appetito!
An Vento
Elyge

RICCIARDI & ASSOCIATI

Design
Antonio Alfani
Francesco Ricciardi

Publisher
Ricciardi & Associati

Graphics and impagination
Simona Mongiu
Maria Teresa Pasquali

Editing
Maria Teresa Amoroso

Cover and all food photography
Eugene Martinez

*All images used to illustrate the recipes
are elaborations of original photographs.*

Photographic archives
Alessandra, Annamaria, Marcella
e Orsola Alfani; Antonio Alfani;
Orsola Lonigo Latour; Francesco Ricciardi.

Everywhere we look, there is a need for help. I believe that it is our responsibility to help others whenever we can.

Part of the proceeds of the sale of this book will be donated to a not-for-profit organization to help a variety of causes. In this way, you and I will be helping in our small way to make the world a kinder place. The recipient will change from time to time.

You can visit my website, www.antonioalfani.com to see who a list of organizations that I am helping thanks to your kind cooperation.

© 2012 Ricciardi & Associati Srl
   00191 Roma - Via del Casale di Tor di Quinto 1
   tel. 06 3336164 fax 06 3336174
   francesco.ricciardi@opra.it

   ISBN 978 88 87525 10 6

www.ricciardiassociati.it

Printed in Italy

Grafica Giorgetti Srl
Via di Cervara 10 - 00155 Rome

TABLE OF CONTENTS

*The recipes are listed, except for a few cases, in the alphabetical order
of their original Italian names.*

The recipes are listed, except for a few cases, in the alphabetical order
of their original Italian names.

Assorted recipes: Vegetables, Frittate and More · 231

The recipes are listed, except for a few cases, in the alphabetical order of their original Italian names.

Desserts

The recipes are listed, except for a few cases, in the alphabetical order of their original Italian names.

INTRODUCTION

By a lucky coincidence, last autumn I had the chance to meet, after fifty years, a distant cousin of mine. He is the author of this book - Antonio Alfani. We hadn't seen each other since I was just a little boy and he was barely a teen. It was the 1950's, we both still lived in Salerno, our home town. Not long after, the ins and outs of life took us on our separate roads and I thought I would never see him again. By the early '60's I was living with my family in Rome, where I would remain all my life, while Antonio departed on a series of experiences that would take him first to Naples and Rome, and later as an adult to Paris, London and New York. Antonio persued his freedom, his instincts, his passions: love, his studies of architecture, art, fashion, textile design and – last but not least – food.

It was in Manhattan that he dedicated himself to the art of cooking, as he followed yet again his instincts – the same ones that had always led him around the world: the search for the best that the culinary arts could offer. It was his family's legacy, jealously guarded and handed down from each generation of skilled cooks to the next, that would call him. It was his decisive moment: from that point on it would be the art of the kitchen that would occupy all of his attention.

Following the pleasure of rediscovering each other after our chance meeting, and beyond our interest in our shared family roots, it was precisely these two elements that brought us to decide to collaborate on the creation of this book: we both are passionate custodians of our family's memories, intent on not neglecting them, cultivating with care our family stories. And both of us share and love, albeit in differing spheres and with differing roles and backgrounds which may seem distant but aren't, the same subject: Antonio, positioned securely and with great skill, in the kitchen and me, a writer and editor who concern himself with that which the kitchen produces. For Antonio this represents a project that has occupied him for some time and that represents for him a synthesis of his own existential experiences – both personal and familial – and the most engaging of all his activities - two aspects of his life that are always intertwined and that remain in constant dialog with each other. This is why I am both touched and honored that he has entrusted me to transfer his passions onto the printed page.

The first chapter, then, is dedicated to the family tales – unusual for a cookbook. They are stories that for the most part revolve around strong women, beginning with the Belgian ancestor, Emilie, and arriving with Lucrezia, Antonio's mother, and the women of the most recent generations. It's no great discovery that it is the women, givers of life, that are the priestesses of continuity and the true witnesses of our family histories – and certainly not only in the kitchen. In the other chapters, Antonio tells, through his recipes, the story of his art in which the relationship with the first part of the book, on the surface apparently subtle, is visceral and deep. Many threads come together in his story and in his recipes – as many as are the passions and experiences of his life – the dominant theme being, naturally, his roots in the South and, of course, his family. The reader who discovers the substance of his recipes will also find them easy to follow. Under Antonio's guidance, even the most complex dish becomes accessible and fun.

About ten years ago, Antonio – who likes to think of himself as a "gypsy of the world" - put down roots. Together with his life partner, Eugene, he has chosen Chianti as his home. But already he's planning new projects and new voyages... I hope they'll be brief. It would be hard for me to wait another half century to meet him again.

FRANCESCO RICCIARDI

PREFACE

The great Marie Antoine Carême wrote, *"When we no longer have good cooking in the world, we'll no longer have literature, nor higher intellect, nor friendly encounters, nor social harmony"*. We can add that good cooking will survive only as long as we continue to have passion and love for the pleasure of giving pleasure - as the author of this book has. His recipes' history comes from afar, carried forward by women from another time, by enterprising men who depart on voyages for the pleasure of discovery and not out of necessity. Like them, Antonio travels, exlores the world and its people in far away places, he works, he learns, he creates. Cooking is his passion – in it, he expresses a way to discover the joy of creating a meeting place for our emotions.

Antonio travels, but a long red thread keeps him tied to the ancient traditions of the foods of his own land. He recalls the memory of the smokey kitchens of his ancestors, those masters of the art of providing a meal with very little, the main ingredients being love and intelligence, or with the finest ingredients imaginable when times were better.

Antonio Alfani unfolds for us a long list of recipes – clear, easy to understand, seductive to the point that we want to immediately try them. He approaches "la grande cucina" through its basic recipes, but then he opens up a wide panorama onto the best food that the Bel Paese has to offer. There is Rome and Sicily, Veneto and Liguria.. But most of all there is Naples and Campania, the lands that our Antonio has always kept in his heart, that neapolitan cuisine that is a concentration of civilization, indeed of the civilizations that bloomed along our Mediterranean coasts and left so many indelible traces.

In Alfani's ample and complete array of recipes, we find his enormous sense of "real" cuisine as an expression of the people, of our people of the fields and of the sea, that grand and intelligent collection of traditions that enables us to say that the many and varied cuisines that comprise the food of our "boot" are great.

This book of Antonio Alfani's can be read as a novel, beginning with the tales of his ancestors and leafing through the recipes as if they were the chapter titles of a long narrative. But its real place is in the kitchen, right alongside your own notebook of family recipes, ready to be browsed and consulted. It's a beautiful and beautifully designed book, but let's not worry if, after some time, we might find a random food stain here and there, or the corners of its pages turned down. This will be the greatest compliment that our Antonio Alfani can receive.

GABRIELE GASPARRO
Rome from Rome
Accademia Italiana della Cucina

UN, DEUX, TROIS...

The Tales

TALES AND RECIPES

"... un, deux, trois - mes petits beignets!
Ditez merci!
In the kitchen, while 'monsù' sleeps, I will tell you the secrets
of all the dishes that I learned from my mother and from my
mother's mother. When we're in the kitchen we only speak in French.
Do you understand, mon chou?", she asked little Angelica.
"Oui maman".

I have a real love for cooking, the basic ingredient of eating well. I inherited this love through the memory of a woman who lived in the 1800's, my father's grandmother, who was born exactly in the middle of that century, in 1851. She was a fine cook and, as we would say today, a great chef - in the sense that not only did she know how to cook, she knew how to direct a whole team of cooks in her kitchen. Emilie - this was her name - was a wonderful cook, not only "her" dishes but those that had come to her from her grandmother who was born at the end of the century before. Until the last years of the 1700's, Emilie's grandmother lived in a little village in the Ardenne, a cold and rainy place so tiny no one even remembers its name. But it wasn't very far from Verviers, the main city of the Vallone regione in the Belgian province of Liege - very close indeed to the German border and to the Low Countries.

On the next page, Emilie at 14 years of age.
On this page, Verviers and its river, the Vesdre,
in an old photograph.

When her husband, a worker in the textile mills, died she found herself alone with her babies to raise and, so, she found herself forced to do what she knew how to do best - spin wool. That's all she would do from the morning until night, and in this way she managed to support her family. In the kitchen, she was expert at turning what little she could find into delightful new treats for the many little mouths that she had to feed. Her daughters would never forget those aromas and flavors and later when they married and had gone to live in places far from Belgium, they would talk among themselves, on those rare occasions when they could get together, of their mother's kitchen. Even Emilie, still only a little girl, would play with the pots and pans, imitating her elderly grandmother who had learned to cook from no one but who had left to her daughters and granddaughters - and especially to her own namesake, Emilie, her love of food.

Emilie's mother, Lucia Deenen, married Alexandre Latour and had five other children as well - Giuseppe, Alfredo, Adolfo, Vittorio and a daughter, Felisì (Felicita). She raised them all with infinite love, instilling in each of them the meaning of family. No wonder, then, that years later, when Emilie entered into the big family of her own husband, Mariantonio Alfani of Salerno, it wasn't difficult for her to win their affection. Alexandre, head of the family, was attracted by a job offer that arrived to him from a Swiss entrepreneur who had, with the blessings of the Bourbon court, established a number of textile mills in the Sarno and Irno river valleys, just to the north of Salerno. Because of the Belgians' fine reputation in the art of textile production, they were highly sought after in these new southern mills. Alexandre's city, Verviers, was at that time a great center of the European textile industry, particularly in wool. It was recognized in all the world, from the twelfth century through the first half of the twentieth, for the refined quality of its products, for its technological innovations and for the skill of its workers.

Alexandre didn't hesitate - he packed up his wife and children, and he left for the deep South where he happily settled. He and his descendants set down their roots in their new home and Belgium, so far away in space and time, became for them a strong yet distant source of strength. The Latour's were tall, their coloring and lineaments bespoke their northern origins - a background as remote to them as it was, and is, still familiar in the family until this day.

At right, the Cotton Textile Mill in Fratte, Irno Valley near Salerno. Above right, Alexanre Latour. Above left, Alexandre's daughter, Emilie, at 18 years of age.

Circa 1890, the Alfani and Latour families.
From the left, standing: Orazio Alfani, Giuseppe Latour, Diego Alfani,
Alfredo Latour (with a glass in his hand), Gerardo Alfani, Marianna Rocco
and her husband Adolphe Latour (wearing the helmet, also in the small photo
to the right) and Vittorio Latour. Seated, from the left: Felicita Latour
with the little Giuseppe Latour Jr., Lucrezia Alfani, Alexandre Latour,
Emilie Latour Alfani, Giulia Scaletta (wife of Alfredo Latour)
with in her arms, Adolfo Latour Jr.

milie Latour, my great-grandmother from Belgium, arrived in Salerno and shortly after entered into what's known as a "good marriage", becoming the wife of Mariantonio Alfani, of the princes of San Cipriano, owners of huge estates in the great plain of the river Sele. That austere southern gentleman was hardly Emilie's contemporary: she was born in 1851, he thirty years earlier. He was more or less the same age as her father, Alexandre. Surely he was "old", but this didn't worry Emilie. She was happy with her groom and, as Signora Alfani, she found herself at the head of large family – the owners of villas, stupendous gardens, farms and orchards and breeders of thoroughbred horses, cattle and sheep. Very quickly did Mariantonio learn to respect his young bride and to find in her the kind of wife he'd always yearned for, capable of steering his family in the right direction. This little Belgian girl turned out to be the perfect lady of the house in what was one of the grand families of the South. She even managed to have her new husband agree to opening up a great arch in the wall between two rooms of their palazzo on the main boulevard of the city, so that on holidays the entire family could sit together at one very long table: the Alfanis, all the in-laws and all their friends. Very often, the members of her own family, the Latours, would join in their festivities. By then, some of the Salerno Latours had made great advances in textiles while others had entered into other successful enterprises, like her brother Adolphe, who became a successful hardware merchant in nearby Naples.

*Late 1800's (circa 1885), the Farina brothers. Orsola, the youngest,
would marry Orazio, one of Emilie's sons.*

onna Emilie was not only the absolute head of the household, she was most importantly the head of the kitchens. Her second in command was the monsù. The kitchen of every "good" family in the South was under the direction of the monsù – a figure evolved from the French "monsieur" in the 1700's, he was the chef, the master of the kitchens. Under Emilie's direction, the unfailing monsù, with the help of a team of women, prepared luncheons and dinners that were a symphony of flavors: delicacies from Belgium, France, Naples. The Belgian "pallini di riso in brodo" (page 119) alternated with the Neapolitan "timballo di maccheroni" (page 170), the northern "capon in butter sauce" (page 192) with the very Mediterranean "sausages with broccoli rabe". And what can we say about those delicate "ramaquins" (page 281), perfect to savor before sitting down before a succulent "tagliolini gratinati ai funghi porcini"? The velvety sauce of "carne alla glace" (page 194), the woodsy flavors of the "tronco di castagne" (pag. 296) - dishes prepared and offered for the delight of the Alfanis, the Latours and their friends?

ven today in my cooking classes, my students are won over when we begin with those tasty ramaquins, which never make it to the table because they're "intercepted" as soon as they leave the frying pan! These ramaquins have traveled for over two centuries and many

countries since Emilie's grandmother prepared them in the Verviers countryside. Hers were without prosciutto or cheese, because she couldn't afford such extras - instead she would add a touch of honey. Try making them without eggs - you'll have the famous "zeppole" known throughout the Spanish Quarters of Naples and the Vicolo dei Barbuti in Salerno - a simple, "poor" treat. The people of the world meet each other and find common ground through their cuisines - their breads with or without leavening, the pizzas with their many names and forms, or the dishes based on meats cut into small pieces and cooked with potatoes, spices or vegetables. Call it a stew, goulash or peposo - the only thing that changes is the creativity of the chef.

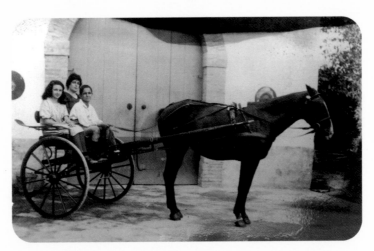

Tavernanova (circa 1925): Orazio Jr. and Giannina with their mother, Orsola.

The Alfani owned large tracts of farmland in the Sele Plain. These huge farms were subdivided into large lots, called masserie in the South. Their biggest masseria was Tavernanova. It was a paradise, one where Emilie spent a great part of her summers. She loved to walk along the shores of the Sele, where they would sit and listen to the music of the river's movement and of the magnificent nature that surrounded them - oak forests, pastures and farmland. Emilie's orchards bore fruit of every kind: lemons, peaches, oranges and apples... fruits that accompanied so well the bounty of her vegetable gardens that were tended so knowingly by her peasants. The water buffaloes, raised free range among the many springs of the river plain, gave fresh milk for the butter that would be prepared at dawn - along with the fresh eggs from her hens and the honey from her bees... and the chocolate she had sent from Belgium - these were the ingredients she used to prepare her exquisite pastries. Mariantonio, in love with his young wife, would murmer to her in his affectionate and protective way, "bambolina mia" - my sweet little doll, and together they had ten children. It came to be that Donna Emilie found herself with less and less time to dedicate to her kitchen. Now she had to give her attention to her many children and their French and German nannies. She decided that as soon as her daughters would be old enough, she would pass the command of the kitchen to them, to accustom them to the duties and responsibilies, once they were grown up and married, of

their own households. Like all the young ladies of "good society" of those times, her girls learned to embroider, to play the piano, to draw and paint. Every day, a quantity of madeleines would come out of Emilie's ovens - delicious pastries with the fragrence of lemons, to offer any friends who would stop by to visit. No one ever left without a package of those treats, tied up with a red ribbon.

Donna Emilie – by this time this is how she was referred to, in Italian, or else "eccellenza", like her husband. But the young woman, finding herself in a role she felt was larger than she, would always blush. Now and then, with the help of her mother-in-law, Carolina, and one of the nurses, she would be able to dedicate herself to the kitchen, at least when there were particularly important guests like the Marquis Farnia and his wife, of whom the Alfanis and the Latours were especially fond. Years later, Orazio Alfani, their third born and the carrier of the family name, would marry a daughter of the marquis, the proud and refined Orsola Farina, who in the first half of the 20th century was one of the most celebrated personalities in Salerno. Succulent dishes were always on the table at the elegant luncheons held in the family's palazzo in Salerno or at their villa in Baronissi, and their fragrances reached all the way to Naples, where the family of the marquis' brother, the Senator Mattia Farina and his wife, the austere "marquise" Olga (as she was called) often invited Orsola and

In the small photo, Orazio Alfani, Sr.

her four children. The little ones loved their uncle and their aunt, who had the ramaquins al formaggio prepared for them according to the recipe handed down from Emilie.

1903, Villa Farina in Baronissi: Orsola is standing behind her mother, Amalia, with her sister Olga, at left, and her brother Mattia, Senator of the Kingdom.

Emilie liked to tell about how her mother, every now and then, would go to Paris to visit her old friend, Jeanne Weil, with whom she would enjoy stopping at the Patisserie des Deux Gourmandes for tea, to exchange news of their families and to talk about their common passion for the kitchen. Jeanne was the wife of Adrien Proust, a renowned physician. During their chats, the two friends would talk about the conquests of their oldest sons, Marcel and Gerardo. The madeleines were the favorite sweets in both households; in fact it was their fragrance that inspired Marcel, in his adult years, when he began to write his "Recherche". And it was Jeanne who passed the secret of these delicate pastries to Emilie, and to reach me, a century later, to reprise her original recipe and to enjoy creating new variations: with chocolate, sour cherries in rum, pistachios, pine nuts...

When they resided in the city, in Salerno, during the good weather, don Mariantonio and donna Emilie would go out for long walks with their children and with Aunt Felicita, along the lovely seafront promenade. Later they would stroll along Via Mercanti - the main street of the city's old quarter. There they would stop in at Salerno's most

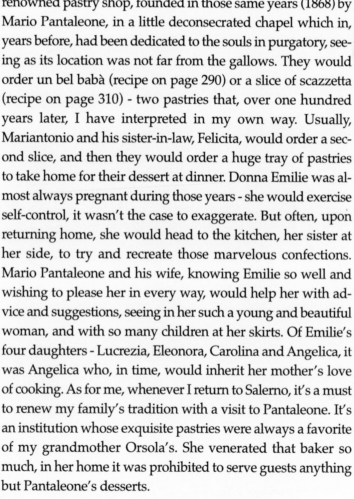

renowned pastry shop, founded in those same years (1868) by Mario Pantaleone, in a little deconsecrated chapel which in, years before, had been dedicated to the souls in purgatory, seeing as its location was not far from the gallows. They would order un bel babà (recipe on page 290) or a slice of scazzetta (recipe on page 310) - two pastries that, over one hundred years later, I have interpreted in my own way. Usually, Mariantonio and his sister-in-law, Felicita, would order a second slice, and then they would order a huge tray of pastries to take home for their dessert at dinner. Donna Emilie was almost always pregnant during those years - she would exercise self-control, it wasn't the case to exaggerate. But often, upon returning home, she would head to the kitchen, her sister at her side, to try and recreate those marvelous confections. Mario Pantaleone and his wife, knowing Emilie so well and wishing to please her in every way, would help her with advice and suggestions, seeing in her such a young and beautiful woman, and with so many children at her skirts. Of Emilie's four daughters - Lucrezia, Eleonora, Carolina and Angelica, it was Angelica who, in time, would inherit her mother's love of cooking. As for me, whenever I return to Salerno, it's a must to renew my family's tradition with a visit to Pantaleone. It's an institution whose exquisite pastries were always a favorite of my grandmother Orsola's. She venerated that baker so much, in her home it was prohibited to serve guests anything but Pantaleone's desserts.

Aunt Felicita with one of her nephews, Giuseppe.
Above, Corso Garibaldi, Salerno in the early 1900's.

Angelica Alfani at 16 years of age.

hen Angelica was eighteen years old, she was invited to go to Paris by Jeanne Proust, who advised Angelica's parents that to let her study painting and cuisine in the City of Lights would be an opportunity for such an intelligent and versatile young woman to have an interesting and formative experience. And so it came to be that Angelica frequented a course in cooking in the kitchens of Auguste Escoffier, and in drawing in Montparnasse. Her brother, Diego, and Aunt Felicita accompanied her on the journey to Paris, where after they left her on her own, she found lodging with the nuns of Sacre Coeur. As chance would have it, soon after her arrival there, Madame Proust, Marcel's mother, passed away. Angelica's compassionate support for Marcel moved him – he grew fond of the young girl as if he were her father. It was he who, one day, introduced Angelica to a man her same age, André – a promising young abstract artist who shared her love of cooking. An immediate "feeling" bloomed between the two eighteen-year-olds, and an innocent love was born.

The young artist's friend and patron was Gertrude Stein, so it was natural that she would want to meet Angelica. She invited the girl to frequent her famous salon, where painters such as Matisse, Braque and Picasso were at home. A horizon opened for Angelica that, in her far away city in the South would never have been available to her. Occasionally, with André's help and that of Fernande Olivier, young Picasso's lover at the time, Angelica would prepare intimate dinners for Stein's troupe: ramaquins al formaggio, capon in butter sauce, babà and profitérols. Only when Pablo cooked a paella was Fernande not allowed to enter the kitchen. Theirs was a tempestuous relationship - the only way to keep them from arguing was to keep her out of the kitchen and him in it! But Angelica's presence was accepted in that minefield, and so it was that she learned how to prepare the dish that is the symbol of Spanish cuisine. Gertrude was happy to surround herself with such talented youth as Angelica and André, who represented to her a welcome distraction from those passionate and endless artistic disputes that she conducted with the likes of Matisse, Henri Rousseau, Alice B. Toklas and with her own brothers, Leo and Mike, with his wife, Sarah.

On this page, Gertrude in 1903, Matisse at work,
a portrait of Matisse by Derain
and a young self-portrait by Picasso.

ngelica would return to Salerno two years later. The time had come for her to start preparing for her future life as the fiancée of the man her parents had chosen for her - Adolfo Latour, her cousin of the same age. Playmates as children, theirs was a love at first sight. The brief affair with André concluded naturally: it would always remain for Angelica just what it was and as it should, a sweet memory.

Angelica and Adolfo Latour.

ngelica's husband and cousin, Adolfo, was a devoted companion during their long life together.
He loved to listen to the stories she would tell their children,
and he was crazy for her tagliolini gratinati (recipe on page
168) and for her exquisite "Sacripantino" (page 320). I have
wonderful memories of this aunt. Once, at her house on my
ninth birthday, she presented me with an enormous block of
chocolate that she had brought back with her on one of her
trips to Paris. I still think back to that generous gesture made
to me by someone so much older than me. My grandfather's
sister will always be in my heart. Of all of Emilie's daughters,
Angelica was the one who was closest to her and the one to
whom she taught all the arts that a girl of that time should
master: needlework, music, running a household... and as far
as the kitchen was concerned, she was capable of teaching her
own teacher! Later, when Angelica became a mother herself,
she would tell her own children bedtime stories about Marcof-
fio - the man in the moon, about Maria 'a longa, or about the
little dog, Sacripante, and Peppinella, his mistress. Angelica
dedicated her favorite creation, the "sacripantino", to this
sweet little dog.

When they were little, Angelica and her brothers and sisters would laugh until they cried when their mother would sing to them this popular little tune: "Cicerenella teneva 'no gallo, tutta la notte 'nce jeva a cavallo, essa 'nce jeva po' senza la sella, chisto è lo gallo de Cicerenella. Cicerenella mia sì bbona e bella...". They would laugh especially giddily when their mother, instead of Cicerenella, would insert the names of Angelica, Lucrezia, or Diego. Sometimes Emilie would forget and sing the song, naming Alderisio, her little son who died at no more than eleven years old, and this would make her sad. But the children were happy to hear the name of their little brother who was no longer with them, and they would hop and jump, singing, "Risio... Risio... Risio...". On occasion, their father would appear, who by then on in his years, was no longer able to keep up with their antics. Instead, he would sit in his big chair, surrounded by his children, and sing to them the song of Cicerenella. But inevitably, he would be swept away by their laughter, and forgetting his years, wind up with them, rolling on the carpet, his little "puppies" climbing all over him. Emilie and Mariantonio's hearts were full of joy with this, their beautiful family.

Donna Emilie always encouraged her children to swim in the river Sele. The boys would go together with their cousins and friends, while the girls could only go with the other girl cousins and friends, and only when accompanied by their Aunt Felicita. For these outings, donna Emilia would order a great basket of snacks to be prepared for them. During the Easter holidays, the family would stay at La Torretta, one of the largest masserie along the river, an ancient hunting lodge that had belonged to the Borbon family that don Mariantonio had acquired at the prospect of having his large family.

Among the brothers, Gerardo and Orazio felt that in some way they should protect Diego, who they often saw aloof and to himself. Even though he always smiled, he never participated in their games and in the many activities that they enjoyed. Diego preferred to stay in the kitchen to busy himself helping monsù and the women of his staff. Diego loved to make pizzas, always inventing new ways to top them. He loved to bake cakes and make marmalades and preserves. Even donna Emilie, worried about this son who was so different from his brothers, had spoken to her husband about him. His response was that Diego should only be left in peace to be himself, to follow his own path, and that the most important thing for him was that his son should only be happy – which is exactly what came to be of Diego, who grew up to live joyously between Naples and Paris. It happened that one day, donna Emilie, stopping to admire the wild ducks and her swans as she strolled with her sister, Felicita, along the shores of the river (her first couple of swans had been a gift from the marquises Farina), she heard festive cries arriving from a nearby grove. A young girl ran out from the thicket, dressed in donna Emilie's wedding gown, chased by a group of boldly nude young men! When the two women realized that the bride was none other than Diego, they didn't know whether to laugh or cry. Donna Emilie had always had her suspicions, but she'd never known what to make of them. She thought of her Diego, who as a child would be horrified to be present for the branding of the young buffaloes, preferring to keep himself apart and play with his sisters' dolls.

Emilie adored her children, but her husband was her heart and soul. She watched him age and thought with melancholy of the time when he would eventually leave her. Certainly she could never be alone, with so many children, her sister and brothers, her father Alexandre, still living, and her elderly mother-in-law Carolina, who had come to love her with all her heart as if she were her own daughter. But without don Mariantonio, she though of her life as a dried up branch.

Orsola Farina at eighteen years of age (1898).

milie was a woman of austere tastes. She always dressed with sobriety and never wore jewelry, not even those splendid jewels given to her by her mother-in-law, donna Carolina Petroni, who was pleased to see her son married to this young girl, slightly contrary, always sweetly respectful yet with an iron will of her own. Only on few occasions was she seen wearing her priceless pearl earrings: certainly at the wedding of her son Orazio with Orsola Farina but not for that of Gerardo and Guglielmina Cioffi, his cousin. After all, it was in the family - no need to show off.

At Tavernanova with some of the Pellegrini cousins. Guglielmina Cioffi is the second from the left. Gerardo, with moustache and wearing a hat, is under the arch.

That Gulglielmina, wife of her firstborn son, hadn't given her any grandchildren was, for Emilie, a disappointment. But the responsibility of continuing the line fell on her youngest son. Orazio and Orsola had four children. Don Mariantonio would never meet their youngest - a sudden sickness took him away at the young age of thirty-three years. For donna Emilie, it wasn't her first heartache to be accepted in silence. She had already lost a son, Alderisio, at eleven years old, and then little Giovanna - they called her Giannina - who died horribly from the burns caused when a gas lamp fell on her dress. Like her brother Alderisio, Giannina was only eleven when she died. It was then, while little Giannina struggled to survive, that don Mariantonio, by then over eighty years old but still a horseman, fell from his horse. Donna Emilia found herself attending her poor dying child while with a forced smile, calming her injured husband. Giovanna's death preceded her father's only by hours - the news of his daughter's accident was too much for him to bear - he never recovered. In the end, they both left Emilie alone. Only some years later would donna Emilie begin to smile again when her daughter-in-law Orsola, widowed of her beloved Orazio, entrusted her, her brother and sister-in-law Gerardo and Guglielimia, with the care of her four little ones. Only then did Emilie return to life, and in her life there was always... her cooking.

At left, little Giovanna, known as Giannina,
who died in tragic circumstances.

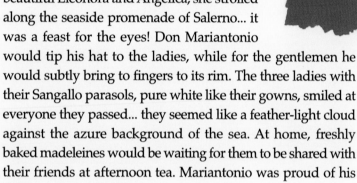

Lying in bed, when she was half asleep, Emlie would think back to the times, so many years before when, along with Mariantonio and their beautiful Eleonora and Angelica, she strolled along the seaside promenade of Salerno... it was a feast for the eyes! Don Mariantonio would tip his hat to the ladies, while for the gentlemen he would subtly bring to fingers to its rim. The three ladies with their Sangallo parasols, pure white like their gowns, smiled at everyone they passed... they seemed like a feather-light cloud against the azure background of the sea. At home, freshly baked madeleines would be waiting for them to be shared with their friends at afternoon tea. Mariantonio was proud of his family, which he received as if they were a gift from heaven when he, at 47 years of age, had finally decided to settle down.

Salerno's seaside promenade at the time our story takes place.
The photograph is from 1902.

As he grew older, Mariantonio took to thinking about the events of his life, about his city of Salerno at the beginning of the 1800's, about his lands and about the bandits with which the countryside was so thick. He would think about the time when, riding home from one of his masserie with his his foreman, his carriage was stopped by a group of thugs on horseback. It became clear that they intended to kidnap him. But right away they realized that he wasn't the man they were after - they let him free with a profusion of excuses and apologies. But the fright for Mariantonio was the same - he knew that at home, his young wife, pregnant with their firstborn and ready to give birth from one moment to the next, waited for him. By the time he reached Salerno, little Gerardo, beautiful and full of life, had already arrived. The luncheon at the Alfani house to celebrate the baby's baptism would be remembered in Salerno and in the entire Sele Plain. Over eighty guests from the family alone were there and the dessert was a babà over one meter in diameter - the invention of Felicita with the help of monsù and the women of the kitchens. A babà that big had never been made before!

Donna Emilia had been in mourning for too many years over the deaths of Alderisio, Giovanna and her husband. For her son, Orazio's, wedding to Orsola Farina, donna Emilie, desired a great celebration, even grander than

On the facing page, Orsola with her daughter, Giannina.
On this page, the Farina family in 1898.
Orsola is the second from the left.

Gerardo and Guglielmina's wedding party. For this son, she decided to organize something at Palazzo Alfani that would be remembered for years to come. The festivities began three days before the wedding, which would be celebrated in the Cathedral of Salerno by the archbishop himself. The reception held the night before featured donna Emilia's most splendid and excellent dishes, prepared for her by the monsù. At the grand ball that followed the dinner, it was Angelica's youthful charm that stole the spotlight from the bride. But Orazio and Orsola were happy. Even donna Emilie danced with her sons and with senator Farina. By now she was over fifty, but she still had the smile of a girl. For the occasion, she wore, for the first time in her life, an emerald green gown and her spectacular pearl earrings. But in her heart, the children and beloved husband, who she had lost, were still alive. Emilie couldn't know that destiny had in store for her another heartache - the death of her son, Orazio, only eight years later.

             amma Lina - Orsola Farina had ordered her grandchildren to call her in this way. She hated the word "grandmother". It made her feel old. She had rules that she applied to every single moment of her day. When we grandchildren went to visit her, exclusively upon her invitation, her lady-in-waiting would let us in and show us to a small sitting room filled with Victorian furnishings. After some

At left, Orazio Alfani Sr. with his wife Orsola and their children Mariantonio, Alfonso and Giovanna (Giannina). Their fourth child, Orazio Jr., wasn't yet born – his father would never know him. Circa 1913.

minutes, she would arrive. After allowing us to kiss her hand, she would concede to each of us an icy kiss on the cheek. While her thoughts were always spiritual, she could never wrap her arms around us in an affectionate embrace. She would always commend me: if my father should fall ill, to call the priest, immediately. When I look at the photographs of her as a young girl, pretty and sweet as the marzipan that she loved so much, it's hard to think of her as a cold woman. Perhaps Guglielmina, the one granddaughter that she loved and who loved her... perhaps she is the one person who really knew my grandmother.

Once a year and only once, in the month of June, Mamma Lina would set an elegant table and invite one of her sons and his family. So my family would be invited every four years. She would receive each daughter-in-law with a formal handshake, and at the end of the visit she would dispatch them with "farewell". I can still remember the menu of one of these excellent luncheons, deserving of the family culinary tradition: gratin of tagliolini in the manner of Angelica, carne alla glace with ramaquins and for dessert, a beautiful babà with pastry cream and wild strawberries. Served by two ancient butlers in their white uniforms. Only once, Pina, the first wife of Mamma Lina's son Alfonso, lost her composure and

threw a box of chocolates at her mother-in-law... but she had been provoked!

Donna Orsola, involved in her other interests, had drifted slightly from the attention of her family. Now and then she would appear - severe, often angry with her children who, growing up, would always demonstrate great affection for their mother but also for their grandmother and uncles and aunts who were the ones who really looked after them. No one ever forgot – we even talk about it today of the time when donna Orsola burst into Villa Alfani in Pontecagnano, just outside Salerno, where her three sons, by then adults, had organized an elegant dinner party with Josephine Baker as the guest of honor. Irritated because they hadn't consulted her first, in a fit of rage she tore the tablecloth from table, with all its sumptuous settings, sending crystal and porcelain flying everywhere. What did she want, this mother, always praying for their souls in the family chapel under the guidance of a Franciscan brother for whom she had a particular affection? Only after the pious monk's death did donna Orsola allow herself to distance herself, slowly, form her constant prayers and consent to marry the solicitor Falvella, who had always been in love with her.

Orsola Farina Alfani with her four children,
Mariantonio, Alfonso, Orazio and Giannina.

hen no one was watching, donna Emilia would dry her tears... her heart still filled with ancient aches. But when an enchanting little girl was born to her eldest grandson, Mariantonio, and his wife, Clelia, she was so happy that she decided that she shouldn't be overwhelmed by her sad memories. Her last years were to be untroubled, dedicated to the care of her grandchildren and not only to her prayers. And her best times would be in the kitchen, alongside the cook, where she would devote herself to preparing her recipes for her big family. When, in 1934, she joined her husband and children who had preceded her, Emilie had a peaceful smile on her lips.

ike her mother, Angelica was also a woman with a strong character. Angelica was an attentive and affectionate mother to her six children who, together with her husband, she raised with great care, teaching them self-respect and to follow their best instincts. Her four sons would follow splendid careers and give her a battalion of grandchildren, whom Angelica would remain devoted to her entire life. I'll never forget when my uncle Alfredo, Angelica's oldest, who would go often to London on business, came to visit us. He brought me a little toy double-decker bus. I was still a child, but I still remember. Of my uncle Renato, I still have his cheerful smile before my

eyes. And of his two daughters, both of them rightful interpreters of the family culinary tradition, the eldest, Aunt Giulia, married Roberto Petroni, a judge and nephew of the philosopher Benedetto Croce. Giulia liked to crochet and created delightully original handbags to give to her sisters, cousins and sisters-in-law. She was the hostess of refined tea parties, always served with great elegance by her uniformed butler. Aunt Giulia was a refined cook - when we went to her house for lunch, we loved her special pallini di riso in brodo (recipe on page 119). Aunt Rosaria married Enrico Ricciardi, a great professional, third generation in a dynasty of engineers - his father realized important buildings in

The 1920's - Angelica with her daughers Maria Rosaria (in her arms) and Giulia. Above, the 1960's - Angelica with her grandchildren Germano and Antonio, Rosaria's. sons.

Naples and Ravenna while the Palace of Justice in Rome and the thermal baths of Agnano were built by his grandfather. In the 1950's. My father, Mariantonio, asked Enrico to design our county home for us - an interplay of white cubes inspired by rationalist architecture. The house was admired by all our friends.

Maria Rosaria Latour Ricciardi.
Above, with her husband, Enrico.

Mariantonio Alfani.

ariantonio, my father, was donna Orsola's first born. He and his brothers, Alfonso and Orazio, enjoyed a carefree youth as "young gents", spoiled by their uncles and by their grandmother Emilie. The three young men, between games of roulette and baccarat, cabaret dancers, race horses, Alfa Romeos and Bugattis, jaunts to Paris and Casablanca... were the envy of their peers as they shared their life of leisure with their closest friends and cousins. In spite of his marriage and the birth of his daughter, Mariantonio continued to lead his carefree lifestyle. Eventually, he drifted from his wife and the young Guglielmina, who grew up pampered and loved, but only by her mother and her grandmother Orsola. When she became an adult, Gulglielmina would, in her turn, be a devoted mother to her family and her three daughters.

Family Photo in the green countryside of the Sele Valley.
From left: Mariantonio and Clelia, a friend, Mamma Lina,
Giannina and Orazio.

In those years, Tavernanova was an enormous farm. Along with the traditional crops and the herds of buffalo (in the mid 1880's, Gerardo Alfani had been one of the first to develop the raising of buffalo for mozzarella in the Sele Plain), the Aflani had established a sophistcated horse-breeding stable of the "Persano" cavalry horse, a breed originally from that area between Battipaglia and Paestum. Tavernanova was the center of that area known as Persano and since time immemorial had provided the military with their horses. The Alfanis, along with some other families of horse-breeders in the Plain – the Farinas, the Moreses, the Moscatis, the Bellellis – sensing a potential beyond the breed's military use, crossed it with an English thoroughbred line, giving birth to an authentic new halfbreed that came to be known as the "Alfani". In 1932, the crown prince Umberto di Savoia, on an official visit to Salerno, stopped at Tavernanova to admire the famous horses of the Alfani family.

Horses at Tavernanova. On the facing page, 1932, Prince Umberto di Savoia during his visit to the the Alfani horse farm. At his side, Mariantonio, my father.

Some time later, at the beginning of the 1940's, it happened that Mariantonio would meet a beautiful young woman, the daughter of one of his employees - Lucrezia, my mother, with whom he fell hopelessly in love, defying the ire of his mother. Orsola would never approve of any of her sons' wives - none of them could be good enough. Excluding a brief infatuation with a certain Roman lady, theirs was a long and loving marriage. My mother still remembers how, on the rare occasion of even the mildest argument, Papà would insist on making up before they would go to sleep.

Lucrezia.
On the facing page, with Mariantonio at Tavernanova.

Of the brothers, Alfonso was the hedonist. Among his friends there were Luchino Visconti, the Cianos, Emilio Pucci, the shipping magnate Antonio d'Amico who bought the villa, La Torretta, from us. Alfonso and his wife, Kikki, never had time for their children, even if they did give them every luxury. When Antonio d'Amico was in Salerno, he would host dinner parties at his villa in Sala Abbagnano. Sometimes the marquises Frescobaldi would arrive from Florence and on these occasions the elegant pastries of Pantaleone would always be offered - especially the "Scazzetta" for the marquise Bona. And when d'Amico would be a guest of the Oranges at their villa "Elefante Felice" on Mount Argentario in Tuscany, he would have the famous pastry chef of Salerno send that exquisite cake for the pleasure of Queen Giuliana of Holland and the princess Beatrice.

Alfonso (first on the left) with his friends at the track; in uniform with his brother Orazio; Rachele (Kikki) Testaferrata, his wife.

Orazio Jr. in morning dress on the occasion of the wedding of his sister, Giannina. In the small photographs, other moments of his life: his wedding with Marisa; with his friends the Ricciardis and de Bartolomeis' in front of his villa in Pontecagnano; with Giannina and his brother-in-law Aurelio Lonigo.

Once he decided to settle down, the third brother, Orazio, a noted casanova when he was young, became an exemplary husband and father. His Marisa, a woman of great class and beauty, was also an accomplished cook. The mutual affection of their five children (Orsola, Annamaria, Alessandra, Gerardo and Marcella) is a constant reference point for me and for the whole family. In Annamaria, I find the same strength of character as our great-grandmother Emilie.

Marisa Pallotta Alfani.
On the facing page, together with her husband, Orazio.

Giannina Alfani Lonigo

And finally Aunt Giannina, my father's only sister and the gentle wife of count Aurelio Lonigo of Padova, was a good and affectionate mother. Though she'd lived so far from her family in Salerno, she was careful to never lose her own traditions, including the family's culinary history, and handed them down to her own daughters - Emma, Orsola and Vittoria. These were the recipes that she had inherited from Emilie. Of the three, Orsola, who married her mother's cousin, Renato Lonigo, is the image of Emilie. Their only daughter, Emilia, brings new life to the name and memory of our ancestor from Belgium, as in her smile she recalls her father. But this is a tale of today...

Emilia Latour jr

ALFANI FAMILY	**LATOUR FAMILY**

GERARDO
1798 - 1872
CAROLINA PETRONI
1800 - 1870 ca

ALEXANDRE
1809 - 1880 ca
LUCIA DEENEN
1830 - 1880 ca

MARIANTONIO
1820 - 1901
EMILIE LATOUR
1851 - 1934

EMILIE
1851 - 1934

ALFREDO
1855 - 1915 ca
GIULIA SCALETTA
1860 - 1920 ca

FELICITA
1852 - 1920 ca

Giuseppe
Adolfo
Vittorio

GERARDO
1869 - 1942
GUGLIELMINA CIOFFI
1880 - 1840 ca

ORAZIO
1872 - 1913
ORSOLA FARINA
1880 - 1962

Diego Carolina Alderisio Lucrezia
Luigi Eleonora Giannina

ANGELICA
1888 - 1972

ADOLFO
1888 - 1960
ANGELICA ALFANI
1888 - 1972

Giuseppe

MARIANTONIO
1906 - 1972
CLELIA FEDERICO

ALFONSO
N 1909 - 1991
KIKKI TESTAFERRATA

GIANNINA
1911 - 1989

ORAZIO
1913 - 1980
MARISA PALLOTTA

RENATO
1916 - 2003
ORSOLA LONIGO

GIULIA
1918 - 2005

M.ROSARIA
1922 - 1994

Alfredo
Giuseppe
Franco

LUCREZIA
1924

ROBERTO PETRONI

ENRICO RICCIARDI

AURELIO LONIGO

ANTONIO
1942

To help the reader, who no doubt has found it sometimes difficult to unravel the names and characters in this story, I've provided here an essential tree the Alfanis, the Latours and those intimately tied to them.
Of the women of my family whose recipes I refer to, or to whom I am in debt for the knowledge and training I received either directly or indirectly, I've included photographs to give faces to the names.
The alert reader will notice that not only have I noted the marriage of Mariantonio Alfani to Emilie Latour, but also the marriage celebrated, with a regular papal dispensation because of the shared blood lines, of their daughter Angelica and her cousin Adolfo Latour - an event that only served to strengthen the ties between the two families.

ACKNOWLEDGEMENTS

I warmly thank my partner, Eugene Martinez, for photographing my dishes and making them even more succulent and inviting. Heartfelt thanks go to my cousins Orsola, Annamaria, Alessandra and Marcella Alfani of Salerno, and to my cousins Orsola and Emilia Latour of Rome for the wonderful photographs that illustrate the "tales" which are the basis for my cooking. Thank you, too, to my dear cousins Maria Teresa and Francesco Ricciardi, and to their daughter Giulia Elena who brought us together after decades apart and whose rich archive of family photographs they so affectionately put at my disposal.

Eugene with our dachshund, Babù.

To Francesco, who is also my editor, I owe a special thank you because he rendered my book even more beautiful than I could ever have imagined. The tableward that appear in the photographs are from Richard Ginori (Florence), Ceramica Solimene (Vietri-sul-Mare), Margaritelli (Deruta), Arabia (Finland). The decoupage dishes are by Antonio Alfani – that is, me. The ivory and gold dishes are by Richard Ginori from the 1940's and belong to the collection of my mother, Lucrezia Alfani.

I would also like to thank those businesses that operate in the world of food and who have earned my admiration as points of reference and inspiration. I call these the "delights of my life".

Above, Giulia Elena in San Casciano

In the realm of gastronomy: Conti Flavors of Tuscany, in Florence. Near the temples of Paestum (Salerno), Baroness Cecilia Baratta Bellelli's wonderful Agriturismo Seliano. For  pastries and bakery: Pantaleone in Salerno, Curtatone and Fabiani in Florence. For chocolates: Jacques Torres of New York City, Vestri of Arezzo, Gay-Odin of Naples for its unforgettable "Foresta".

Snacks and cocktails are at Varese, in Salerno. In Pontecagnano, just outside Salerno, Filippo Morese (Taverna Penta) produces some of the best fresh mozzarella, while the farm belonging to Piero de Bartolomeis cultivates the most fragrent aromatic herbs which he conserves in glass jars.

When I don't feel like cooking but want to eat well, I choose "Vicolo della Neve" or "Santa Lucia" in Salerno; "Pizzeria Bellini" in the Port'Alba neighborhood of Naples; "Don Alfonso" in Sant'Agata sui Due Golfi (Naples); "Cinque di Vino" in San Casciano Val di Pesa (Florentine Chianti) and in the city of Florence, "La Cucina del Garga",  "Ristorante Totò", "'o Munaciello", "Brasserie Mangiafuoco" and "Il Pizzaiuolo" and "Ciro & Sons".

Basic Recipes

Unless otherwise indicated, the recipes are for 4-6 people

BESCIAMELLA
Béchamel Sauce

Milk	1 qt/1 lt
Butter	7 tablespoons/100 gr
Flour	¼ cup/50 gr
Salt	a pinch
Pepper (if the particular recipe calls for it)	to taste

1. Warm the milk.
2. Melt the butter and add the flour to it all at once.
3. Mix well, then slowly add the warm milk, stirring continuously.
4. Keep stirring until all the milk has been added and the sauce has become velvety. Be sure to eliminate any lumps!
5. Add the salt and pepper.
6. Keep stirring for another minute or two.
7. Turn off the heat, position to sheets of paper towel over the saucepan then cover.
8. Stir the sauce now and then until it has cooled completely so that a skin doesn't form on the surface.

BESCIAMELLA RICCA
Rich Béchamel

Milk	2 cups/ 500 cc
Heavy cream	2 cups/ 500 cc
Butter	7 tablespoons/100 gr
Flour	¼ cup/50 gr
Egg yolks	2, beaten
Salt and pepper	to taste
Freshly grated parmigiano	⅓ cup/100 gr

1. Warm the milk and the cream together.
2. Melt the butter in a saucepan. Add the flour all at once. Mix well.
3. Stirring constantly, add the salt and pepper and the milk.
4. When the sauce has become velvety, turn off the heat.
5. Cover the saucepan. Stir the sauce now and then until it has cooled.
6. Blend in the egg yolks and parmigiano, mixing well.
7. Use right away or keep it, covered, in the refrigerator.

BRODO VEGETALE
Vegetable Broth

Carrots	2, medium	Yellow onion	1
Celery	2 ribs	Cloves	3 or 4
Leeks	2	Fresh flat-leaf parsely	a generous bunch
Garlic	1 clove	Bay leaves	3-4
Pumpkin or butternut squash	100 gr	Black peppercorns	1 tablespoon
		Tomatoes	1 ½cups / 300 gr
Cabbage	¼ head	Saffron	a pinch
Green bell pepper	1	Sale	to taste

- Cover all the ingredients with cold water in a large soup pot. Bring to a boil, then simmer for 3 hours. Strain, adjust for salt.

BRODO DI CARNE
Meat broth

All the vegetables listed above plus:

Beef shank or shin	1 lb / 500 gr	Beef soup bones	as you like
Pork ribs	7 oz / 200 gr	Egg whites	3 or 4, beaten
Chicken wings	4		

1. Cover all the ingredients completely with abundant cold water in a large soup pot and bring slowly to a boil.
2. Before the water begins to boil, pour in a cup of very cold water. This will bring the foam, created by the meat juices, to the surface. Lower the heat so that the pot barely simmers and carefully skim off the foam. This will ensure a clear broth! When no more foam rises to the top, you can stop skimming.
3. Allow to simmer for three hours.
4. Strain the broth, removing the meats to a platter. The meats can be served drizzled with extra virgin olive oil and a squeeze of fresh lemon, or they can be used to prepare delicious meatballs.
5. While the broth is still very hot, pour in the egg whites and allow them to absorb any impurities from the broth. After a few minutes, filter the broth through a cheesecloth and allow to cool. When it's cold, skim off any fat that's risen to the surface.

To make homemade bouillon, cook the broth down to ¼ of its original volume. Let it cool, then pour it into ice cube trays and freeze. The frozen concentrated broth is convenient and easy to use in preparing anything from soups to sauces! To keep them handy, once they're frozen they can be kept in plastic freezer bags.

CREMA AL BURRO E CAFFÈ
Coffee Buttercream

Fresh vanilla beans	1 pod
Sugar	¾ cup / 200 gr
Egg yolks	6
Butter	1 cup / 200 gr
Very strong coffee	1 tablespoon hot and ¼ cup, very cold

1. Cut the vanilla pod in half, lengthwise, and scrape out the beans with a knife. Add the vanilla beans to one tablespoon of very hot coffee for at least 20 minutes.
2. Work the sugar into the butter (allowed to soften at room temperature) until it is perfectly absorbed and the butter has become velvety.
3. Add the the egg yolks one at a time, stirring constantly until they are well amalgamated.
4. Slowly stir in the cold coffee and the vanilla. If you like, you can filter the vanilla from the hot coffee it steeped in and just use the coffee.
5. Place the buttercream in the refrigerator until it solidifies.
6. Before using, take the cream from the refrigerator and allow to stand at room temperature until it's reached a smooth, spreadable consistency.

CREMA AL BURRO E CIOCCOLATO
Chocolate Buttercream

Sugar	¾ cup / 200 gr
Egg yolks	6
Butter	1 cup / 200 gr
Unsweetened cocoa	⅓ cup / 100 gr

1. Work the sugar into the butter until it is perfectly absorbed and the butter has become velvety.
2. Add the egg yolks one at a time, stirring constantly until they are well amalgamated.
3. Sift in the cocoa powder and mix until the buttercream has become a uniform chocolate color.
4. Refrigerate until it solidifies.
5. Before using, take the buttercream from the refrigerator and allow to stand at room temperature until it's reached a smooth, spreadable consistency.

CREMA PASTICCIERA
Pastry Cream

Whole milk	1 qt / 1 lt		Egg yolks	10
Sugar	¾ cup / 200 gr		Peel of one organic lemon	2
Flour	⅓ cup / 100 gr, sifted	*(only the yellow part)*		

1. Heat the milk
2. Combine the the egg yolks and the sugar, then sift in the flour.
3. Slowly stir in the hot milk and the lemon peel.
4. Cook over low heat, stirring constantly.
5. When the cream begins to thicken, lift the spoon from the cream and draw your finger along it. If it leaves a clean trail, the cream is ready.
6. Remove the lemon peels and keep stirring to keep a skin from forming on the surface.
7. When it cools, cover and place in the refrigerator. Chill well before using.

CREMA CHANTILLY
Chantilly Cream

- As above, but when you remove the chilled cream from the refrigerator, delicately fold in 1 ⅓ cup / 300 cc of whipped cream. Keep refrigerated.

GANACHE

Ganache is bittersweet, milk chocolate, or "gianduja"
(milk chocolate mixed with ground hzlenuts) melted into hot heavy cream, then cooled.

Chocolate (milk, bitter or gianduja)	7 oz / 200 gr
Heavy cream	¾ cup / 200 gr

1. Break the chocolate into very small pieces or chop it in the food processor.
2. Bring the heavy cream to a boil, add the chocolate.
3. Stir constantly until you have a dense cream that can be used in a multitude of recipes.
4. To the ganache, you can add ground almonds, pistachios or hazelnuts.
5. Instead of nuts, you can add a liquor such as rum, bourbon, grappa or a bold, full-bodied red wine. In this case, reduce the quantity of heavy cream by the amount of liquor or wine used. For example, if you use ¼ cup 50 cc of cognac, reduce the heavy cream to ½ cup / 150 cc.
6. You can use ganache in any of its variations to make chocolate truffles, candies and cakes!

GENOVESE DI LUCREZIA
Lucrezia's Genovese Sauce

It's best to use a terra cotta pot because it holds the fragrences of the sauce best and doesn't alter its flavors. What's more, it cooks most uniformly.
In absence of terra cotta, a Dutch oven can be used as well.

Beef shank	2lbs/1kg
Extra virgin olive oil	¾ cup/200cc
Garlic, coarsely chopped	2 cloves
Celery, coarsely sliced	4 stalks
Carrots, coarsely chopped	4
Fresh flat leaf parsley	a handful
Bay leaves	6
Salt	to taste
Tomato paste	3 tablespoons
Dry white wine	⅓ cup/100 cc
Yellow onions, coarsely chopped	9 lb/4 kg
Hot water	to cover

1. Heat enough e.v.o.o. to cover the bottom of a Dutch oven. Don't be stingy with the oil - remember, we're in Napoli!
2. When the oil is hot, brown the meat (no salt!), then remove and keep warm.
3. Add the garlic, carrots and celery to the hot oil and sauté for a few minutes.
4. Add the tomato paste dissolved in the wine.
5. Add the onions, parsley and bay leaves. Pour in hot water to cover.
6. Bring to a boil.
7. When it begins to boil, place the meat over the onions, cover the pot and simmer over a low flame for about 3 hours stirring occasionally so that the onions don't stick. If you see that the sauce begins to dry out, add boiling water as necessary.
8. After about 4-5 hours of slow simmering, remove the meat keeping it covered so that it will remain moist. Stir occasionally, making sure that the onions don't stick to the pot.
9. Remove the meat and the bay leaves. Keep the meat warm.
10. Pass the sauce through a food mill then return it to the dutch oven.
11. Add salt to taste.
12. Simmer, uncovered, until the sauce is smooth and creamy.
13. As the sauce finishes cooking, cut the meat into thick slices and return it to the sauce to warm up.

- This sauce is wonderful on long ziti, the kind that you break apart before cooking, or with tagliolini gratin with provola (smoked mozzarella) and tiny meatballs made with the meat from the genovese.

GLACE ALLE FRAGOLINE
Wild Strawberry Glaze

If wild strawberries are not available, tiny cultivated strawberries can be used.

Wild strawberries	1 lb / 500 gr
White wine	1 cup / 250 cc
Confectioners' sugar	1 ⅓ cup / 300 gr

1. Wash the strawberries in the white wine, then drain them.
2. Cook them in a saucepan with the sugar, stirring frequently.
3. Using an immersion blender, reduce them to a purée, then continue cooking until almost as dense as a gelatin.
4. Remove from the heat and allow to cool.
5. The glaze can be kept for a long time in the refrigerator.
6. To ice a cake such as the scazzetta (see recipe on page 310), warm the glaze on the stove or in the microwave. Carefully pour the glaze over the cake, using a small spatula to distribute it on the sides. Let cool, then repeat this two or three times for a perfect icing.

MEZZA FROLLA SALATA
Light Savory Shortcake

This recipe is perfect to make the dough of a classic Timballo di Maccheroni
(see recipe on page 170)

Flour	1 ¼ lb / 600 gr		Egg yolks	2
Sugar	2 oz / 60 gr		Butter	1 ⅓ cups / 300 gr, very cold
Eggs	2 whole		Salt	¾ oz / 20 gr

1. Using a fork, mix together the flour, the sugar and the butter which has been cut into cubes.
2. When you have a crumbly dough, mix in the eggs, the egg yolks and the salt.
3. Mix very well. Avoid using your hands so as not to warm the dough.
4. Form the dough into a small loaf, wrap it in plastic cling wrap and refrigerate for at least 30 minutes.
5. If left longer in the refrigerator, let it sit at room temperature for about an hour before using.
6. Roll the dough out to the thickness you require.

PAN DI SPAGNA

In the 19th century, a chef of the Court of the King of Spain prepared a cake that very much pleased the king, who ordered his own chefs to include this recipe into the court repertoire. From that moment, the cake was known as Pan di Spagna, "spanish bread" and has been considered part of the Spanish tradition ever since.
Pan di Spagna is similar to an american or english sponge cake, but is denser and richer.

Flour	7 oz / 200 gr
Sugar	1 ¾ cup / 300 gr
Eggs	10, separated

1. Beat the egg whites until stiff.
2. In a large mixing bowl, use an electric mixer to beat together the sugar and the yolks.
3. Sift in the flour, folding it gently into the batter with a spatula.
4. Delicately fold in the beaten egg whites, being careful not to deflate them.
5. Pour the batter into a backing pan that has been greased and dusted with flour.
6. Bake for 30 minutes in an oven that's been preheated to 350°F / 180°C / Gas Mark 4.
7. Remove from the oven and allow to rest for 10 minutes.
8. Turn the cake out onto a cooling rack and allow to cool completely.
9. At this point, the pan di spagna is ready to use - slicing it horizontally into layers to be filled with creams and ganaches, or into strips to become a zuppa inglese.

PAN DI SPAGNA AL CIOCCOLATO
Chocolate Pan di Spagna

Flour	⅓ cup / 100 gr
Bitter cocoa powder	¼ cup / 50 gr
Sugar	¾ cup / 200 gr
Eggs	6, separated

- As above, sifting the cocoa together with the flour.
- The quantities of this recipe are smaller than the above recipe for the classic Pan di Spagna, so the cake will come a bit smaller.

PASTA BIGNÈ
Puff Pastry

The bigné was born in Florence where it was called "pasta cotta" or "cooked dough". It was Caterina de' Medici, the future wife of the son of King Francis I of France, who took florentine chefs with her when she moved to Paris, and introduced to the court and, therefore, to France, the specialty that today we think of as so French - the bignè.

Hot water	1 cup / 250 cc
Flour	½ cup / 150 gr
Butter	7 tablespoons / 100 gr
Eggs	4
Salt	a pinch

1. Melt the butter and salt in simmering water.
2. Remove from the heat and add the flour to the hot water all at once.
3. Mix briskly with a wooden spoon until the batter no longer sticks to the sides of the saucepan.
4. Allow to cool. When the batter reaches room temperature, mix in the eggs one at a time. Don't put in the next egg until the one before it has completely amalgamated into the batter.
5. Continue mixing for another few minutes after the last egg has been absorbed.

- At this point the batter is ready to use for a savory preparations such as ramaquins or sweet recipes such as profitérols.

PASTA FRESCA
Tagliatelle, Lagane, Cavatelli, Fresh pasta

Semolina flour	1 cup / 250 gr
All purpose flour	1 cup / 250 gr
Salt	a pinch
Extra virgin olive oil	1 tablespoon
Boiling water	as much as the dough can absorb, about 1 ⅓ cups / 300 cc

1. Mix the two flours together, then form then into a "volcano" on a board or in a large mixing bowl.
2. Pour the water (not all of it) and the oil into the "crater" of the volcano and begin to mix it in with the flour, allowing it to be absorbed until you have a dry, even dough. Your hands will get a little messy but it'll be worth the trouble when you taste the result.
3. Keep mixing for 10 minutes, turning the dough constantly.
4. Form the dough into a loaf, then wrap it in a cloth that's been soaked in cold water then wrung dry.
5. Allow to rest for 30 minutes.
6. For cavatelli, divide the dough and form into "cigars", then cut the cigars into pieces about 1/2" / 1 cm long.
7. Dust them with flour and when all the pieces are cut, begin to roll each piece with a fingertip to give the cavatello its characteristic shape.
8. For tagliatelle or lasagne or lagane, roll the dough out until it's very thin and divide it into squares or strips, or roll up the sheet and slice it as thinly as you like.

PASTA FRESCA ALL'UOVO
Fresh egg pasta

Flour	1 cup/250 gr	Extra virgin olive oil	1 tablespoon
Duram wheat flour	1 cup/250 gr	Salt	a pinch
Large eggs	5, beaten	A little water, if needed	

1. Form the flour into a "volcano" on your work surface.
2. Pour the beaten eggs, the oil and the salt into the "crater".
3. Work the liquid into the flour until it has been well absorbed. Add a little water if you find it necessary to make the dough more pliable. It should be soft but not sticky.
4. Dust the work surface with flour and knead the dough using the heels of your hands.
5. When the dough is soft, elastic and dry form it into a loaf and wrap it in a cloth that's been soaked in cold water and wrung dry. Allow to rest for 30 minutes.
6. Divide the dough into smaller pieces and use a rolling pin to roll it out to the thickness you desire.
7. Dust with flour, then roll the sheet up.
8. Using a sharp knife, slice the rolled up dough to the width you need - thin for tagliolini, wider for tagliatelle, wider still for pappardelle. For cannelloni, don't roll the sheet up - cut it into rectangles to be rolled around the filling of your choice.

PASTA VERDE ALL'UOVO
Green Egg Pasta

All purpose flour	1 lb/250 gr	Large eggs	5, beaten
Spinach	7 oz/200 gr, boiled and drained	Extra virgin olive oil	1 tablespoon
		Salt	a pinch

1. Purée the spinach, drain and press as much of the water out of it as you can.
2. Form the flour into a "volcano" on your work surface.
3. Pour in the beaten eggs, the oil and the salt into the "crater". Work the dough the eggs have been well absorbed.
4. Add the spinach and mix in thoroughly.
5. Dust the work surface with flour and knead the dough using the heels of your hands. Add a little more flour if necessary.
6. When the dough is soft, elastic and dry form it into a loaf and wrap it in a cloth that's been soaked in cold water and wrung dry. Allow to rest for 30 minutes.
7. Divide the dough into smaller pieces and use a rolling pin to roll it out to the thickness you desire. Dust with flour, then roll the sheet up.
8. Using a sharp knife, slice the rolled up dough to the width you need - thin for tagliolini, wider for tagliatelle, wider still for pappardelle. For cannelloni, don't roll the sheet up - cut it into rectangles to be rolled around the filling of your choice.

PASTA FROLLA
Shortbread

All purpose flour	2 ⅔ cups/600 gr
Sugar	1 ⅓ cup/300 gr
Butter	1 ⅓ cups/300 gr, very cold, cubed
Egg yolks	8
Salt	a pinch
The zest of one organic lemon	

1. Use a fork to mix together the flour, sugar and butter. Don't use your fingers as your body heat will warm up the dough.
2. When the dough is crumbly, add the eggs, lemon zest and salt.
3. Mix thoroughly, trying to use your fingers as little as possible so as not to warm up the dough.
4. Form the dough into a loaf, wrap with plastic cling wrap and place in the refrigerator for at least 30 minutes.
5. If the dough is too cold when you are ready to use it, let it sit outside the refrigerator until it achieves the consistency you desire.

- Baking time and temperature of the shortbread depends on the recipe you are preparing.
- To bake cookies, the oven temperature should be high (400°F/200°C/Gas Mark 6) and the baking time brief (about 15 minutes)
- For a tart, the oven temperature will be lower (350°F/180°C/Gas Mark 4) and the baking time longer (about 30 minutes or more)
- For the pastiera napoletana the temperature will be 350°F/180°C/Gas Mark, but the baking time will be as much as 50 minutes.

PASTA GÉNOISE
Genovese Pastry Dough

*This cake was named in honor of the Genovese chef who created the recipe
and was assumed by the Spanish court in the 18th century.
The addition of butter and the working of the dough with heat result in
a cake that is more delicate and flavorful than the simpler "pan di spagna".*

All purpose flour	¾ cup/200 gr
Sugar	1 ⅓ cup/300 gr
Egg	10
Butter	1 ½ tablespoons/20 gr

1. Whisk the eggs together with the sugar in a large mixing bowl that has been placed in a larger pan of gently boiling water, or bain marie.
2. Remove from the heat and whisk in the butter, mixing constantly. When it has cooled, mix in the flour.
3. Beat the egg whites until stiff, then using a spatula, delicately fold them into the batter.
4. Pour the batter into a baking pan that's been previously greased and dusted with flour.
5. Bake for 30 minutes at 350°F/175°C/Gas Mark 4.
6. Remove from the oven and allow to cool.
7. The genoise is now ready to be sliced horizontally in 2 or 3 layers, to be filled with creams or custards.

- Naturally, if you increase the amounts of the ingredients, you'll have a larger cake which you'll have to bake in a larger pan – otherwise it will come too tall and will not have the right consistency.

PASTA MADDALENA
Madeleine Pastry

*This pastry batter is used to make "madeleines", the little shell-shaped pastries
that Marcel Proust remembered in his "Recherche", or for a cake embellished with sour
cherries in rum, grated chocolate, julienned almonds, lemon zest or
whatever strikes your fancy.*

All purpose flour	1 cup/225 gr
Powdered yeast	1 level teaspoon
Sugar	1 cup/250 gr
Egg yolks	12 large
Butter	1 cup/250 gr

1. Melt the butter, then allow it to cool.
2. Mix the egg yolks with the sugar.
3. Sift in the flour and the yeast, mix well.
4. Drizzle in the melted butter, mixing constantly, until the batter obtains a smooth, velvety consistency.
5. Mix in whatever "extras" you like.
6. Place in the refrigerator for a couple of hours before baking.

- For a cake, bake the batter in a cake pan lined with a parchment paper disc for 30 minutes at 350°F/180°C/Gas Mark 4.
- When cooked, remove from oven, allow to cool, then serve dusted with confectioners' sugar.

PASTA PER PIZZA
Pizza dough

All purpose	1 lb / 500 gr	Salt	a pinch
or Manitoba flour		Sugar	a pinch
Fresh yeast cake	1 oz / 25 gr	Warm milk	4 teaspoons/20 cc
Extra virgin olive oil	1 tablespoon	Warm water	4 teaspoons/20 cc
	Room temperature watervas needed		

1. Combine milk, the warm water, the oil, salt and sugar in a mixing bowl, then crumble in the yeast.
2. Allow the mixture to rest until a slight foam has formed on the surface, the sign that the yeast is "active".
3. Form the flour into a "volcano" on your work surface, and introduce the yeast mixture into the "crater".
4. Using a fork, gradually mix the flour with the mixture until all the liquid has been absorbed. Add more room tempreature water as needed.
5. Dust the work surface with flour, and knead the dough for at least 10 minutes.
6. Divide the dough into as many pizzas as you like or need, or divide it into small pieces for pizzette and calzone.
7. Cover and place in a warm location to grow for at least one hour.
8. Flatten each pizza out, either with the hands or with a rolling pin, and allow to rise for another 30 minutes.
9. Preheat the oven to 450°F/250°C/Gas Mark 9 or higher. Baking time depends on the size of the pizza and its toppings, and can range from 15 to 30 minutes.

SALSA DI POMODORO
Tomato Sauce

Ripe San Marzano (plum) tomatoes	2 lb/1 kg
or	
Tomato purée	3 cups/750 gr
Extra virgin olive oil	¼ cup/50 cc
Salt to taste, Fresh basil several leaves	

If you like, you can sauté a thinly sliced onion and a whole clove of garlic

1. Drop the fresh tomatoes into boiling water. When their skins break, remove them from the water. Peel the tomatoes and remove the seeds.
2. Dice the tomatoes or put them through a foodmill.
3. Cook, together with the e.v.o.o., over medium heat for 20-30 minutes.
4. Add salt and the basil.

PASTA SFOGLIA
Flaky Puff Pastry

All purpose flour	1 cup / ½ lb / 250 gr
Soft butter	1 cup / 250 gr, at room temperature
Salt	a pinch
Water	½ cup / 100 cc

1. Form the flour into a "volcano" on your work surface and pour half of the water and a pinch of salt into the "crater".
2. Use a fork to mix the flour into the water, adding more water a little at a time until all the water has been absorbed by the flour.
3. Work the dough until it is soft yet dry. Allow the dough to rest for 15 minutes.
4. Lightly dust the work surface with flour, then using a rolling pin, roll the dough out into a square.
5. Place the butter in the center of the square, then fold the sheet of dough over it to like an envelope.
6. Starting in the center, roll the dough outwards to the edges. Roll back and forth to obtain a rectangle.
7. Turn the sheet 90°, roll out from the center toward the edges, then fold the rectangle into thirds so that there are now three layers.
8. Starting from the center, roll the dough out to form a new rectangle.
9. Turn the sheet 90°, fold it in thirds and roll it out again, always starting from the center and rolling toward the edges.
10. Fold the sheet in thirds and place it in the refrigerator for 15 minutes.
11. Remove from the refrigerator and repeat the operation.
12. Return to the refrigerator for another 15 minutes.
13. Repeat the operation another two or three times before returning it to the refrigerator. After this last time, the dough will be ready to be rolled out into one thin sheet.
14. At this point, the sheet can be stored in the refrigerator until ready for use.
15. Before returning to the refrigerator, you should decide if you will use the flaky pastry on its own or if it will be filled. If the former, poke the entire surface with a fork before refrigerating. A tool is available to do this – it resembles a small rolling pin with pins or spikes, but a fork will do just as well. If on the other hand, you will be filling the pastry, as in a strudel, this step can be skipped.
16. The baking time of the pastry depends on the recipe being followed.
17. An elegant way to decorate the pastry is to use the same dough to form a braided trellis or to cut little leaves and arrange them over the surface, brushing it all with a beaten egg yolk thinned with a little milk.

POLPETTINE DI CARNE
Little Meatballs

Ground beef or mixed beef, pork and veal	10 ½ oz/300 gr
Day-old bread	7 oz / 200 gr, soaked in water then squeezed dry
Eggs	2
Freshly grated parmigiano cheese	¼ cup/50 gr
Extra virgin olive oil	as needed
Salt and pepper	to taste

1. Mix all the ingredients well.
2. Refrigerate for a few hours or overnight.
3. Using a spoon or a small ice scream scoop, form little meatballs the size of a hazlenut. Use your hands to roll them into perfect little balls.
4. Roll well in flour, then fry in very hot olive oil, moving the pan back and forth so that the meatballs will brown evenly.
5. Remove with a slotted spoon to a plate covered with paper towel to absorb the oil.
6. Use the meatballs right away in recipes such as pasta al forno (baked pasta) or timballo di maccheroni. Otherwise they can be kept in the refrigerator for up to three or four days.

- If you happen to have the meat that was used to prepare a ragù or a genovese, you can use it instead of the ground beef or mixed meats. This will result in a more delicate and tasty meatball. Naturally, in this case you'll use the sauces to dress whatever dish you're preparing with the meatballs!
- Using this same recipe, instead of making tiny meatballs you can make large meatballs the size of an egg. Roll them in your hands to form the balls, then after rolling them in flour, gently squash them so that they are somewhere between a ball and a patty.
- Whether they are large or small, the meatballs will last longer stored in sauce.

RAGÙ NAPOLETANO - 'o raù
Neapolitan ragù

Beef shank	2 ¼ lbs / 1 kg
Pork ribs	4
Prosciutto	7 oz / 200 gr, both the lean and the fat, in one single piece
Extra virgin olive oil	as needed
Tomato purée	2 ½ - 3 qt / 2 ½ - 3 lt
Tomato paste	3 ½ oz / 100 gr
Garlic	2 cloves
Onion	1, sliced
Dry white or red wine	½ cup / 100 cc
Salt	to taste

1. Brown the meats (except for the prosciutto) in the e.v.o.o. along with the garlic and the onion.
2. Remove the onion and garlic when they've become golden.
3. Dissolve the tomato paste in the wine, add it to the meat and let it pick up their flavors.
4. Add the tomato purée.
5. When it comes to a boil, cover and reduce the flame until the sauce is barely simmering.
6. Check to make sure that the meats don't stick to the bottom of the pot, stirring occasionally and adding water if necessary.
7. The ragù will have to cook for about about 4-6 hours! About halfway through, add the prosciutto in one piece. At this point, you can remove the cover or continue to cook with the cover slightly ajar until the sauce is creamy and velvety.

- Use this most exquisite sauce in its most classic way, with the long ziti (candele) which are broken by hand so that the sauce envelopes not only the ziti but the tiny bits of pasta that result from the breaking... or a pasta al forno (baked ziti), or a sartù di riso!

First Course:
Pasta, Rice, etc.

Unless otherwise indicated, the recipes are for 4-6 people

BUCATINI ALLA MATRICIANA

I'll refer to the Roman definition of this dish, "Matriciana", and not to the more commonly used "Amatriciana", since it seems the recipe has been verified as having been born in Rome as a variation of "Gricia" - a dish eaten by ancient Roman shepherds made of guanciale (pork jowel) and pieces of sausage.

Bucatini pasta	1 lb / 500 gr
Guanciale or pancetta	3 ½ oz / 100 gr, diced
Onion	1, sliced
Garlic	2 cloves, chopped
Tomato filets	1 ¼ cup / 200 gr
Hot chili pepper	to taste
Aged pecorino cheese, freshly grated	2 tablespoons
Extra virgin olive oil	as needed
Salt	to taste

1. Slowly brown the guanciale or pancetta in the e.v.o.o. over medium-low heat so that the fat will melt into the oil. When it becomes crisp, remove and set aside.
2. Sauté the onion in the hot fat. When it becomes transparent, add the garlic and hot chili pepper.
3. When the garlic begins to turn golden, add the tomato filets and cook over medium heat for about 10 minutes.
4. Return the guanciale or pancetta to the pan, stir and cook for another few minutes.
5. Cook the pasta in salted water and remove quite al dente. Drain, then pour into the pan with the sauce and continue to sauté for several minutes, tossing constantly to cover all the pasta with the sauce.
6. Sprinkle the grated pecorino into the pasta, toss well and serve.

SUGGESTED WINES:
Cerveteri Rosso Asciutto DOC - Lazio
Controguerra Cabernet DOC - Abruzzo

CALAMARATA COL CAVOLFIORE
Calamarata with cauliflower

"Calamarata" is a type of pasta that looks like calamari rings

Calamarata	10 ½ oz / 300 gr
Extra virgin olive oil	as needed
Fresh cauliflower	1 large
Onion	1 large, thinly sliced
Garlic	2 cloves, chopped
Tomato paste	2 tablespoons
Dry white wine	half a glass
Salt	to taste
Hot chili pepper	to taste
Oregano	a pinch
Grated parmigiano	½ cup - 100 gr

1. Sauté the onion and garlic in the e.v.o.o.
2. Add the hot chili pepper. After allowing it to sautè with the garlic and onion a bit, add the tomato paste which has been dissolved in the wine.
3. Break the cauliflower into pieces about the size of a walnut and add to the sauce-pan. Stir, add salt to taste and oregano. Cover with boiling water.
4. Cook the cauliflower for a few minutes, then mix in the pasta and enough water to cover it. Cook the past together with the cauliflower. If necessary, as the pasta cooks and absorbs the water, add a little more - enough so that by the time the pasta is cooked the sauce will be creamy smooth.
5. When the pasta is cooked al dente, remove from the heat, cover and allow to rest for 5 minutes.
6. Remove from the flame and allow to rest for 5 minutes.
7. Serve with a drizzle of e.v.o.o. and freshly grated parmigiano.

SUGGESTED WINES:
Torgiano bianco - Umbria

CALAMARATA ALLA NORMA
Calamarata with eggplants

A popular Sicilian dish, dedicated to the composer of the opera, Norma, Vincenzo Bellini

Penne, Calamarata or Ziti	1 lb / 500 gr
Eggplants	2 ¼ lb / 1 kg, cut into 1/2" / 1 cm cubes
Fresh mozzarella or salted ricotta	7 oz / 200 gr, grated
Grated pecorino cheese	3 1/2 oz / 100 gr
Peeled tomatoes, deprived of their seeds	1 lb / 500 gr
Garlic	1 clove, crushed
Fresh basil	2 tablespoons, chopped
Extra virgin olive oil	as needed
Salt and pepper	to taste

1. Place the cubed eggplant in a non-stick pan, no oil, over a low flame and allow to lose its liquid, stirring and tossing constantly for several minutes. Remove.
2. Heat enough e.v.o.o. in the pan to fry the eggplant cubes in small batches. As the eggplants become golden, drain them on paper towel to absorb the excess oil.
3. When all the eggplant are done, pour off any excess oil from the pan leaving a couple of tablespoons. Add the tomato filets and sauté along with the garlic for 10 minutes.
4. Mix in the eggplants, salt and half of the chopped basil.
5. While the sauce was cooking, the pasta will have boiled in abundant salted water. Drain al dente and toss into the sauce.
6. Serve the pasta on warmed plates, topped with the cubed mozzarella or grated ricotta salata and sprinkled with chopped basil and freshly grated pecorino cheese.
7. When the pasta is cooked and dressed, serve it on warmed dishes. Over each dish of pasta arrange a few spoonsful of the cubed fresh mozzarella and a generous sprinkling of grated ricotta salata.

SUGGESTED WINES:
Contea di Sclafani Pinot Nero DOC - Sicily

CANNELLONI CON CARNE
Meat cannelloni

FOR THE PASTA:

see page 77   12 squares

FOR THE BÉSCHAMEL:

see page 66   1 cup/250 cc

FOR THE TOMATO SAUCE:

see page 81   1 qt/1 lt

FOR THE FILLING:

Boiled ham	5 ½ oz/150 gr, ground
Ground beef	5 ½ oz/150 gr
Ground pork	5 ½ oz/150 gr
Garlic	1 clove, finely chopped
Onion	1 medium, chopped
Dry wed wine	¼ cup/50 cc
Extra virgin olive oil	¼ cup/50 cc
Salt and pepper	to taste

1. Cook the pasta squares in abundant salted water. When they are al dente, drain and arrange on a large cloth that has been soaked in water and wrung dry. This will keep them from sticking.
2. Sauté the onion and garlic in the oil.
3. Add the meats, salt, pepper and the ground boiled ham.
4. Cook the meats, stirring frequently, but don't brown them.
5. When cooked, allow to cool then mix in the béschamel and two tablespoons of tomato sauce.
6. Fill the cannelloni being sure to not overstuff them so much that the filling comes out the ends.
7. Spread a thin layer of béschamel on the bottom of a baking dish, then place the cannelloni in the dish, packing them in snuggly but not too tighly.
8. Cover with the tomato sauce, sprinkle generously with grated parmigiano and bake for 20 minutes at 150°F/180°C

SUGGESTED WINES:

Aglianico del Taburno Rosso DOCG - Campania

CANNELLONI RICOTTA E SPINACI
Ricotta and Spinach Cannelloni

FOR THE PASTA:

see page 77	12 squares

FOR THE TOMATO SAUCE:

see page 81	2 cups / 500 cc

FOR THE RICH BÉSCHAMEL:

Ricetta a pag. 66	2 cups / 500 cc

FOR THE FILLING:

Ricotta	1 ¾ cups / 300 gr
Spinach purée	1 ¾ cups / 300 gr
Eggs	2
Extra virgin olive oil	2 tablespoons
Grated parmigiano	1/2 cup / 100 gr
Garlic	1 clove, chopped
Salt and pepper	to taste
Breadcrumbs	¼ cup / 50 gr
Butter	¼ cups / 50 gr

1. Cook the pasta squares in abundant salted water. When they are al dente, drain and arrange on a large cloth that has been soaked in water and wrung dry. This will keep them from sticking.
2. Mix the tomato sauce with the béschamel to obtain a creamy pink sauce.
3. Sauté the spinach and the garlic in a little e.v.o.o.
4. In a mixing bowl, mix together the spinach, the ricotta, the eggs, the salt and pepper, and half of the parmigiano. Mix in 2 tablespoons of the pink sauce.
5. Arrange 2 tablespoons of filling on each pasta square, then roll up the pasta into a tube, making sure that no filling comes out of the ends.
6. Grease a baking pan and dust it with breadcrumbs. Arrange the cannelloni in the pan, snugly but not too tightly. Cover generously with the pink sauce. Top with the rest of the grated parmigiano, salt and pepper.
7. Bake for 30 minutes at 400°F / 200°C / Gas Mark 6.

SUGGESTED WINES:
Locorotondo bianco DOC - Puglia

CANNELLONI SOGLIOLA E PORRI
Canneloni with Sole and Leeks

FOR THE PASTA:
see page 77   12 squares

FOR THE BÉSCHAMEL:
see page 66   1 qt/1 lt

FOR THE FILLING:

Leeks	1 lb/500 gr, thinly sliced
Sole filets	14 oz/400 gr
Extra virgin olive oil	¼ cup/50 cc
Garlic	2 cloves, chopped
Dry white wine	¼ cup/50 cc
Breadcrumbs	¼ cup/50 gr
Butter	¼ cup/50 gr
Salt and pepper	to taste

1. Cook the pasta squares in abundant salted water. When they are al dente, drain and arrange on a large cloth that has been soaked in water and wrung dry. This will keep them from sticking.
2. Sauté the leeks and garlic in the e.v.o.o. Add the wine.
3. When the leeks are cooked, add the sole filets and, using a fork, break them apart.
4. Add salt ane pepper to taste.
5. Allow to cool, then mix in 1/3 of the béschamel.
6. Fill each cannellone with 2 spoonsful of filling. Roll them up, being sure not to let the filling squeeze out from the ends, and arrange them snugly in a baking dish that's been greased and sprinkled with breadcrumbs.
7. Cover with the rest of the béschamel and bake for 30 minutes at 400°F/200°C/Gas Mark 6.
8. Serve very hot.

SUGGESTED WINES:
Greco di Tufo bianco DOCG - Campania

CANNELLONI PORCINI E SPECK
Cannelloni with porcini mushroom and speck

Speck is a salt cured and lightly smoked ham from the Alto-Adige Subtirol.
Today it's popular in all regions of Italy.

FOR THE PASTA:

see page 77	12 squares

FOR THE BÉSCHAMEL:

see page 66	1 qt / 1 lt

FOR THE FILLING:

Dried porcini mushrooms	⅓ cup / 3 ½ oz / 100 gr
Lean speck or smoked Canadian bacon	7 oz / 200 gr, cut into very small cubes
Fontina cheese	7 oz / 200 gr, cut into tiny cubes
Butter	3 ½ tablespoons / 50 gr
Extra virgin olive oil	¼ cup / 50 gr
Spring onions or shallots	6 medium
Dry white wine	½ cup / 100 cc
Eggs	2
Fresh flat leaf parsley	1 tablespoon, chopped
Grated parmigiano	½ cup / 100 gr
Salt and pepper	to taste

1. Soak the dried porcini in warm water. When they are tender, drain, squeeze dry and chop finely. Sautè the porcini along with the shallots in the butter and e.v.o.o. When the shallots become transparent, add the wine and reduce.
2. Mix the cooked mushrooms with the speck and the fontina.
3. Mix in part of the béschamel, the grated parmigiano, salt and pepper.
4. Spread a small amount of béschamel on the bottom of a baking dish.
5. Cook the pasta squares in abundant salted water. When they are al dente, drain and arrange on a large cloth that has been soaked in water and wrung dry. This will keep them from sticking.
6. Place a couple of spoonsful of filling along the length of each pasta square. Roll up the square around the filling to form the cannelloni.
7. Arrange the cannelloni snugly in the baking dish.
8. Cover abundantly with béschamel and more grated parmigiano.
9. Bake at 400°F / 200°C / Gas Mark 6 for 20 minutes or until a delicate crust has formed on the surface.

SUGGESTED WINES:
Aglianico del Taburno DOCG (red) - Campania
Colli di Bolzano DOC (red) - Trentino Alto Adige

CAVATELLI AL RAGÙ

*Cavatelli are "dumplings" hand rolled from a very simple form of pasta.
Typical of the entire South of Italy, they come originally from Campobasso,
in Molise, where the most traditional way to serve them is with ragù.*

FOR THE PASTA:

All purpose flour	1 lb/500 gr
Very hot water	about 1 ¼ cups/300 cc
Olive oil	1 tablespoon
Salt	a pinch

FOR THE RAGÙ (OR SIMPLE TOMATO SAUCE)

See recipe on page 84 (81)	1 qt/1 lt

1. Form the flour into a "volcano" on your work surface. Put a pinch of salt and the spoonful of olive oil in the "crater", then slowly pour in the hot water, a little at a time, using a fork to mix it into the flour.
2. As the water is absorbed by the flour, you can begin to work the dough with your hands, kneading it for about 10 minutes, adding water or flour as necessary until the dough is soft and dry to the touch, not sticky.
3. Soak a clean cloth in water and wring dry. Wrap the dough in the damp cloth and allow it to rest for half an hour.
4. Divide the dough into pieces the size of an egg. Using your hands, roll each piece out into a "cigar" about 1/2"/1 cm thick.
5. Dust the rolls with flour, then cut them into pieces about 1/4" / ½ cm long. In so doing, your cavatelli will be about the size of a hazelnut.
6. As you cut the dough into pieces, spread them on a board that's been dusted with flour. When all the dough has been cut into pieces, begin to form the cavatelli using your index finger to push into the center of the piece and roll it out on the board. The word, cavare, in Italian means to "scoop out", which is what your index is in effect doing. The pasta you form will look like little shells, and the "scoop" will hold the sauce!
7. Cook the cavatelli in boiling salted water for about 30 minutes. They're ready when they are soft yet chewy.
8. Serve with a hearty ragù or, if you prefer, a simple tomato sauce, freshly grated parmigiano and black pepper.

SUGGESTED WINES:
Cannonau di Sardegna (red) DOCG - Sardegna

FRITTATA DI ZITONI DI ROSARIA
Rosaria's frittata di zitoni

A dish invented to make the best use of leftover pasta...
from the recipe of Maria Rosaria Latour Ricciardi

Penne or other pasta	1 lb / 500 gr
Eggs	8, beaten
Fresh flat-leaf parsely	1 tablespoon, chopped
Grated parmigiano	½ cup / 100 gr
Coursley ground black pepper	1 tablespoon
Salt	to taste
Extra virgin olive oil	as needed

1. Mix the cooked pasta with the eggs, salt, pepper, parmigiano and parsley.
2. Allow to rest for 5 minutes, mix again then cook in a non-stick pan that has been lightly greased with the e.v.o.o. Cook over high heat for 2-3 minutes, the cover, lower the heat and cook for another 6-7 minutes.
3. Use the pan's cover to flip the frittata over: holding the panhandle in one hand and the cover firmly over the pan with the other, flip the pan upside down. Remove the pan and position it under and to the side of the cover, allowing the frittata to slip delicately back into it.
4. Allow the frittata to become golden brown then cover, remove from the heat and allow to rest for 5 minutes.
5. Serve hot or at room temperature

SUGGESTED WINES:
Lacryma Christi bianco DOC - Campania
San Severo Bianco DOC - Puglia

GNOCCHI ALLA SORRENTINA

Gnocchi as they are served in the Southern seaside town of Sorrento

Potato gnocchi, see recipe on page 100	1 ¾ lb / 800 gr
Fresh mozzarella	1 ¾ cups 7 oz / 200 gr, cubed
Tomato sauce, see recipe on page 81	1 qt / 1 lt
Extra virgin olive oil	¼ cup / 50 cc
Fresh basil	20 leaves
Salt	to taste
Freshly grated parmigiano	½ cup / 100 gr

1. Cook the gnocchi in boiling salted water. As they float to the surface, remove them to a large mixing bowl, using a slotted spoon or skimmer.
2. Put the cooked gnocchi in a large bowl and dress them with ¾ of the tomato sauce.
3. Place a spoon or two of the cubed mozzarella in each person's dish. Sprinkle with chopped fresh basil and a spoonful of tomato sauce.
4. Cover the mozzarella with the hot gnocchi, covered with a spoonful of hot sauce. Garnish with mozzarella cubes and three fresh basil leaves.
5. Serve hot, sprinkled on top with grated parmigiano.

SUGGESTED WINES:
Greco di Tufo DOCG (white) - Campania

GNOCCHI DI PATATE
Potato gnocchi

Yellow potatoes	2 ¼ lb / 1 kg
Eggs	2
All purpose flour	14 oz / 400 gr
Salt	to taste

1. Boil the potatoes with their skins in abundant water. When they can easily be pierced with a sharp knife, drain and peel them. Pass the potatoes through a food mill or potato masher while they are still hot.
2. Allow to cool, mix in the eggs, the salt and half the flour.
3. Mix and knead well until the dough is soft and uniform.
4. Divide the dough into 10-15 pieces of equal size.
5. Using your the palms of your hands, roll each piece out on a board that's been dusted with flour, until you have a long "cigar" about 1/2"/1 cm wide.
6. Dust with flour, cut the "cigars" into pieces about 1/2"/1 cm long.
7. Lightly dust the pieces with flour, then roll each piece along a cheese grater or the tines of a fork with the fork facing away from you. This will create the little ridges on the gnocchi which will hold the sauce!
8. Place the rolled gnocchi on dishes that have been dusted with flour. This will make it easier later to gather them when it's time to cook them.
9. Bring an abundant pot of salted water to the boil. When the water boils and all the gnocchi are ready, put them into the boiling water a plateful at at time. Be ready with a slotted spoon or skimmer to remove the gnocchi to a warmed bowl as they float to the top of the boilng water.

- Gnocchi can be served with basic tomato sauce or ragù (see recipes on page 81 and 84), or in a butter sauce infused with sage, grated parmigiano and freshly ground black pepper.

SUGGESTED WINES:
Lacryma Christi del Vesuvio DOCG (red) - Campania

GNOCCHI GRATINATI AL TARTUFO
Gnocchi Gratin with Truffles

Potato gnocchi (see recipe on page 100)	1 lb/1 kg
Mozzarella	7 oz/200 gr, cubed
Truffles	¾ to 1 oz/20-30 gr
Butter	½ cup/100 gr
Fresh sage leaves	10 tender leaves, sliced julienne
Grated parmigiano	½ cup/100 gr
Breadcrumbs	¼ cup/50 gr
Heavy cream	1 cup/200 cc
alt and pepper	to taste

1. Cook the gnocchi in abundant boiling salted water. As they rise to the surface, remove them to a large bowl using a slotted spoon or skimmer.
2. Lightly sauté the sage in half of the butter. When they've infused the butter with their flavor, mix in the cream and the cooked gnocchi. Add half of the parmigiano, salt, pepper, the mozzarella and the truffles which have been very thinly sliced.
3. Pour the gnocchi into a baking dish that's been previously greased with butter and dusted with the breadcrumbs.
4. Cover with breadcrumbs mixed with the rest of the parmigiano and dots of butter.
5. Bake at 400°F/200°C/Gas Mark 4 for 30 minutes.

SUGGESTED WINES:
Colli Martani Grechetto DOC (white) - Umbria

IGNUDI DI SPINACI E RICOTTA
Spinach and Ricotta Dumplings

A typical Tuscan 'primo' or first course, ignudi are similar to spinach and ricotta
ravioli but ... nude - without the pasta!

Fresh ricotta, preferrably from sheeps' milk	1 ⅓ cups / 10 ½ oz / 300 gr
Cooked chopped spinach	1 ⅓ cups / 10 ½ oz / 300 gr
Flour	⅓ cup / 100 gr or more as needed
Freshly grated parmigiano	½ cup / 100 gr
Egg	1
Salt and pepper	to taste
Butter	½ cup / 100 gr
Fresh sage	as you like, sliced very thinly

1. Mix the first six ingredients together.
2. Refrigerate for at least two hours.
3. Using two spoons, form a dumpling about the size of a walnut, passing it back and forth from one spoon to the other.
4. Gently place the ignudi into boiling salted water. As they rise to the top of the water, remove them carefully with a slotted spoon and place in a pan in which the sage has infused the warm butter.
5. Serve portions of 4-5 ignudi topped with grated parmigiano and freshly ground black pepper.

SUGGESTED WINES:
Lacryma Christi del Vesuvio DOCG (red) - Campania

INSALATA DI RISO
Rice salad

Rice	10 ½ oz/300 gr
Carrot	½ cup/100 gr, diced and cooked al dente
Green peas	1 cups/200 gr, cooked
Pitted green olives	½ cup/100 gr, sliced
Capers	4 teaspoons/20 gr, washed in tepid water of their salt or brine
Anchovy filets	4, chopped
Cherry tomatoes	2 cups/200 gr, cut in half or whole if they're very small
Tuna in olive oil	7 oz/200 gr, drained
Extra virgin olive oil	½ cup/100 gr
White wine vinegar	1 tablespoon/15 gr
Fresh flat leaf parsley, chopped	1 tablespoon
Salt and pepper	to taste

1. Cook the rice in abundant salted water. When it is al dente, rinse it under cold running water to stop the cooking process. Drain well.
2. Put the rice in a large glass bowl so that you and your guests will be able to enjoy the salad's festive colors.
3. Combine the rice with the flaked tuna, the e.v.o.o., vinegar, olives, capers, carrots, peas, anchovies, tomatoes and parsley.
4. Refrigerate for at least one hour before serving, adding salt and pepper sparingly.

SUGGESTED WINES:
Gambellara DOC (white) - Veneto

INSALATA FREDDA DI PASTA
Cold pasta salad

Pennette or fusilli pasta	10 ½ oz/300 gr
Cherry tomatoes	1 ½ cups/300 gr
• Fresh arugula, washed and dried	1 cup/7 oz/200 gr
• Fresh scallions, sliced	3
• Fresh goat cheese	7 oz/200 gr in cubes
• Extra virgin olive oil	¼ cup/50 cc
• Aged balsamic	a few drops
• Salt and pepper	to taste

1. Cook the pasta in abundant salted water and drain under cold running water when it's al dente.
2. Mix together all the ingredients but the salt and the balsamic. Place the pasta salad, covered, in a cool fresh place until you are ready to serve it.
3. At the last moment, add salt to taste and finish a few drops of excellent aged balsamic and a "thread" of e.v.o.o.

SUGGESTED WINES:
Molise Novello DOC (red) - Molise

LAGANE CON I CECI
Lagane with chickpeas

*One of the most ancient forms of pasta, from the deep south of Italy.
Always home made, served best with lentils, beans, tomato sauce or,
most traditionally, chickpeas.*

Lagane, see recipe on page 76	1 lb / 500 gr
Dried chickpeas	1 lb / 500 gr, soaked overnight in water then boiled for one hour
Pork fat	½ cup / 3 ½ oz / 100 gr, very finely chopped
Fresh flat leaf parsley, chopped	2 tablespoons
Garlic	2 cloves, thinly sliced
Extra virgin olive oil	¼ cup / 50 cc
Salt and pepper or hot chili pepper	to taste

1. Sauté the garlic in the pork fat and the e.v.o.o.
2. Add the cooked chickpeas.
3. Cook together for 15 minutes, then mash 1/3 of the chickpeas using a fork or the back of a wooden spoon.
4. Add the salt and pepper or hot chilis and the parsley.
5. Cook the lagane in abundant salted water. When done, drain, add to the chickpeas and sauté for a few minutes, tossing constantly.
6. Serve with grated parmigiano and freshly ground black pepper or hot chili pepper.

SUGGESTED WINES:
Gambellara Bianco DOC - Veneto
Bolgheri Rosato DOC - Toscana

LAGANE CON LE FAVE
Lagane with fava beans

Lagane, see recipe on page 76	1 lb/500 gr
Fresh fava beans, shelled and with their skins removed	1 lb/500 gr
or	
Dried fava beans, soaked and cooked	1 ½ cups/10 ½ oz/300 gr
Pancetta	5 ½ oz/150 gr, diced
Garlic	2 cloves, chopped
Extra virgin olive oil	¼ cup/50 cc
Fresh flat leaf parsley, chopped	1 tablespoon
Grated parmigiano	3 ½ oz/100 gr
Salt ane pepper	to taste

1. Dried fava beans must be soaked in cold water for 12 hours then boiled in their water for an hour. Allow them to cool, uncovered, before using them as you would fresh fava beans.
2. Render the pancetta in the hot e.v.o.o. Add the garlic and sauté. Add the fava beans, salt and pepper.
3. When the pancetta begins to sizzle again, mix well and toss in the lagane which will have been cooked in salted water and drained.
4. Toss in the chopped fresh parsley.
5. Serve with grated parmigiano and freshly ground black pepper.

SUGGESTED WINES:
Locorotondo DOC (white) - Puglia
I Pàmpini Enotea Rosato - Campania

LASAGNE DI VERDURE
Vegetable Lasagne

Lasagne, see recipe on page 77	14 oz / 400 gr
Béchamel sauce, see recipe on page 66	1 qt / 1 lt
Provola (smoked mozzarella), thinly sliced	7 oz / 200 gr
Carrots	3
Celery	2 stalks
Onions	2
Garlic	3 cloves
Dry white wine	½ cup / 100 cc
Fresh mushrooms	10 ½ oz / 300 gr
Dried porcini mushrooms	¼ cup / 1 ¾ oz / 50 gr
Butter	3 ½ tablespoons / 50 gr
Extra virgin olive oil	¼ cup / 50 gr
Grated parmigiano	1 cup / 100 gr
Salt and pepper	to taste

1. Soak the dried mushrooms in warm water for 30 minutes, then drain, wring dry, chopped finely and added to the other vegetables which have all be chopped or diced. Thinly slice the fresh mushrooms
2. Sauté the vegetables in the e.v.o.o, add half the wine and reduce over medium heat. Add salt and pepper to taste.
3. Cook the lasagne in abudant salted water, drain and arrange on a cloth that has been soaked in water then wrung dry. This will prevent them from sticking to each other.
4. Spread a little bit of béchamel on the bottom of a baking dish.
5. Arrange a layer of lasagne over the béchamel, then cover with a little more béchamel.
6. Mix a couple of spoonsful of béchamel with the sautéed vegetables, then distribute the vegetables evenly over the lasagne along with the sliced provola.
7. Arrange the remaining lasagne over the vegetables, cover with the béchamel and sprinkle with grated parmigiano.
8. Bake at 350°F / 180°C / Gas Mark 4 for 45 minutes or until a nice golden crust has formed on the surface.
9. Remove from the oven and allow to rest for 30 minutes before serving.

SUGGESTED WINES:
Trebbiano di Romagna DOC (white) - Emilia Romagna
Montecarlo Bianco DOC - Toscana

LASAGNE VERDI FUNGHI E TARTUFO
Green Lasagne with Mushroom and Truffles

Green lasagne, see recipe on page 77	14 oz/400 gr
Bèschamel sauce	1 qt/1 lt
Mixed fresh mushrooms	1 lb/500 gr, thinly sliced
Dry porcini mushrooms	¼ cup/1 ¾ oz/50 gr
Extra virgin olive oil	¼ cup/50 cc
Butter	½ cup/5 oz/150 gr
Garlic - 2 cloves, slightly crushed	
Fresh truffle	to taste
Fresh mozzarella, cubed	7 oz/200 gr
Grated parmigiano	½ cup/100 gr
Salt and pepper	to taste

1. Cook the lasagne in abudant salted water with a spoon of olive oil. When the pasta is al dente, remove from the water with a slotted spoon or skimmer and arrange on a cloth that has been soaked in water then wrung dry. This will keep the lasagne from sticking to each other. Cover with another damp cloth to keep them from drying as you prepare the sauce.
2. Sauté the garlic in the butter and e.v.o.o.
3. Add the porcini mushrooms which have been previously soaked in tepid water for 30 minutes, drained, squeezed dry and chopped. Add the fresh mushrooms and cook for 10 minutes over high heat in order that they lose their water, tossing and stir constantly.
4. Spread a couple of spoonsful of béschamel on the bottom of a baking dish.
5. Dress half the lasagne with half the béschamel and arrange in the dish.
6. Spread the cooked mushrooms and the sliced mozzarella. Cover everything with the thinly sliced truffle.
7. Cover with a couple of spoonsful of béschamel and the rest of the lasagne.
8. Sprinkle the surface with grated parmigiano.
9. Bake at 400°F/200 °C/Gas Mark 6 for 30 minutes.

SUGGESTED WINES:
Bardolino Rosso DOC - Veneto

LASAGNE NAPOLETANE
Lasagne Neapolitan Style

Lasagne, see recipe on page 76	14 oz/400 gr
Ragù, see recipe on page 84	1 qt/1 lt
Little meatballs, see recipe on page 83	10 ½ oz/300 gr
Mozzarella	7 oz/200 gr, thinly sliced
Neapolitan salami	3 ½ oz/100 gr, diced
Hard boiled eggs	4, sliced
Grated parmigiano	½ cup/3 ½ oz/100 gr
Salt and pepper	to taste

1. Cook the lasagne in abundant salted water. When al dente, use a slotted spoon or a skimmer to remove from the pot and arrange on a cloth that has been soaked in water and wrung dry. Lay another damp cloth over the pasta - this will keep it from sticking to each other.
2. Spread a few spoonsful of ragù on the bottom of a baking dish, then arrange a layer of lasagna over it. Cover the lasagne with a couple of spoonsful of ragù.
3. Distribute over the ragù the salami, the hard boiled eggs, the meatballs. Cover with the sliced mozzarella. Spread a layer of ragù over the filling, and sprinkle with parmigiano.
4. Arrange the remaining lasagne dressed with ragù.
5. Sprinkle generously with parmigiano, salt and pepper to taste. Bake at 400°F/200°C/Gas Mark 6 for 30 minutes.
6. If you prefer a thicker lasagne, use this same amount of ingredients in a smaller baking dish or increase the amount of the ingredients. In either case, bake this larger lasagne at 350°F/180°C/Gas Mark 4 for 45 minutes.
7. Allow the lasagne to rest for 15-20 minutes before serving.

SUGGESTED WINES:
Aglianico del Taburno Rosso DOCG - Campania

LASAGNETTE CARCIOFI E SPECK
Lasagnette with artichokes and speck

Egg lasagnette, see recipe on page 77	1 lb/500 gr
Béshamel sauce, see recipe on page 66	1 qt/1 lt
Artichokes	2 ¼ lb/1 kg
Speck	7 oz/200 gr, finely diced
Fresh mozzarella	7 oz/200 gr, thinly sliced
Extra virgin olive oil	¼ cup/50 cc
Garlic	2 cloves
Grated parmigiano	½ cup/3 ½ oz/100 gr
Breadcrumbs	¼ cup/50 gr
Butter	1 ¾ tablspoons/25 gr
Salt and pepper	to taste

1. Cook the lasagnette in abudant salted water. When they are al dente, remove them using a slotted spoon or skimmer to a cloth that's been soaked in water then wrung dry. Cover with another damp cloth. This will prevent the lasagnette from sticking to each other.
2. Have no pity whey you clean the artichokes! Remove all of the tough leaves, breaking them off until all you have left is the tenderest core. Then cut the artichokes in half and slice them very thinly.
3. Sautè the artichokes in the e.v.o.o. with the garlic and a pinch of salt, tossing frequently so that they don't stick to the pan. When they are tender, remove the garlic.
4. Grease a baking dish with the butter and sprinkle it with the breadcrumbs.
5. Toss the lasagnette with the béchamel, keeping about a cupful of the sauce to the side.
6. Arrange half of the lasagnette in the baking dish. Distribute the artichoke and speck filling and the mozzarella over the pasta. Sprinkle with half the parmigiano.
7. Cover with the remaining lasagnette, the rest of the béschamel, sprinkle with parmigiano, salt, pepper and dots of butter.
8. Bake at 400°F/200°C/Gas Mark 6 for 30 minutes.

SUGGESTED WINES:
Sannio Falanghina DOC (white) - Campania

ORECCHIETTE CON LA ZUCCA
Orecchiette with pumpkin

Fresh orecchiette	1 lb/500 gr
Pumpkin or butternut squash	1 ¾ lb/800 gr, cubed
White onions, thinly sliced	4
Extra virgin olive oil	½ cup/100 cc
Garlic	2 cloves
Fresh flat-leaf parsley, chopped	1 tablespoon
Hot chili pepper	to taste
Salt	to taste
Grated parmigiano	¼ cup/50 gr

1. Sauté the garlic and onion in half of the e.v.o.o.
2. Add the pumpkin or squash and sauté over medium-high heat, only enough for it to begin to take on the flavors of the garlic and onion but not enough that it begins to fall apart. Add salt and the chili pepper.
3. Cook the orecchiette in abundant salted water. When al dente, drain and add them to the pumpkin.
4. Toss well, drizzle with the other half of the e.v.o.o., mix in the grated parmigiano and the parsley.
5. Cover and allow to rest 5 minutes before serving.

SUGGESTED WINES:
Albana di Romagna Secco DOCG (white) - Emilia Romagna

ORECCHIETTE CON BROCCOLI DI RAPE
Orecchiette with broccoli rabe

Fresh orecchiette	14 oz/400 gr
Broccoli rabe, only the most tender parts	1 lb/500 gr
Potatoes, in small cubes	10 oz/300 gr
Extra virgin olive oil	as needed
Garlic, thinly sliced	4 cloves
Hot chili pepper	to taste
Salt	to taste

1. Cook the broccoli rabe al dente, drain, then sauté the e.v.o.o. along with the garlic and hot chilis.
2. While the broccoli is cooking, boil the orecchiette in abundant salted water. 6-7 minutes before they are al dente, add the cubed potatoes.
3. Drain the pasta and potatoes, add them to the broccoli, which have been coarsley chopped once cooked, and sauté for another 5-6 minutes.

SUGGESTED WINES:
Galatina Negroamaro DOC (red) - Puglia
San Severo Bianco DOC - Puglia

PACCHERI AL RAGÙ ALLE 3 CARNI
Paccheri with 3-meat Ragù

Paccheri are huge jumbo-size smooth pasta tubes, similar to rigatoni but without the ridges and much larger. They are the favorite of any true napolitano.

Paccheri	1 ¼ lb / 600 gr
Ground beef	3 ½ oz / 100 gr
Ground pork	3 ½ oz / 100 gr
Ground wild boar	3 ½ oz / 100 gr
Tomato paste	3 ½ oz / 100 gr
Peeled, seeded roma tomatoes	1 lb / 500 gr, chopped
Pancetta	1 ¾ oz / 50 gr, diced
Extra virgin olive oil	¾ cup / 150 cc
Onion	1 large, finely chopped
Garlic	3 cloves, finely chopped
Dry red wine	½ cup / 100 cc
Salt and pepper	to taste
Fresh bay leaf, rosemary and sage, tied into a bouquet	
Grated parmigiano	½ cup / 100 gr

1. Sauté the onion and the garlic. Add the pancetta. When the pancetta fat has rendered, add the ground meats, crumbling them with the back of a mixing spoon.
2. Cook the meats for 15 minutes, mixing frequently.
3. Add the bouquet of herbs.
4. When the meats have browned, add the tomato paste which you've dissolved in the wine. Mix it in with the meats, being sure to scrape the bottom of the pan to loosen the meat if it's begun to stick.
5. Add the peeled tomatoes, crushing them with your hands, along with their juice. If you need more liquid, add hot water.
6. Cook, covered, for an hour over medium heat, stirring frequently. Then uncover and continue cooking until the sauce thickens.
7. Cook the paccheri in abundant salted water. Real paccheri take at least 20 minutes to cook! When they are al dente, drain then toss them with the sauce. Hold aside enough sauce to spoon over each dish when serving.
8. Cook the paccheri with the sauce for a few minutes before serving with a spoon of the steaming sauce and plenty of grated parmigiano.

SUGGESTED WINES:
Montepulciano d'Abruzzo DOC - Abruzzo
Cerasuolo Rosato DOC - Trentino Alto Adige

PALLINI DI RISO IN BRODO DI GIULIA
Giulia's Little Rice Balls in Broth

From the recipe of Giulia Latour Petroni

Meat or vegetable broth, see recipe on page 67	2 qt/2 lt
Arborio or originario rice	1 lb / 500 gr
Eggs	4
Grated parmigiano	½ cup/100 gr
Fresh flat leaf parsley	a bunch, very finely chopped
Breadcrumbs	1 cup/200 gr
Extra virgin olive oil	as needed
Salt and pepper	to taste

1. Cook the rice in just enough water that by the time it is cooked all the water will have been absorbed.
2. Drain well, then spread out in a large, low mixing bowl to cool.
3. When the rice has cooled, add to it the eggs, salt and pepper, parsley and parmigiano. Use a fork to lightly beat the eggs and mix them in with the other ingredients.
4. To form the little rice balls, wet your hands with cold water then shake the water off so that they are just damp - this will keep the rice from sticking to them. Take a small bit of the rice and roll it into a ball about 1/2"/1 cm in diameter.
5. As you make the little balls, place them on a platter on which you've spread out half of the breadcrumbs. When you've made all the rice balls, sprinkle the other half of the breadcrumbs over them.
6. The rice balls should be very well breaded so at this point, rinse and dry your hands and roll them in your palms to be sure that the breadcrumbs stick securely.
7. Arrange them in an orderly manner on the platter.
8. Fry the rice balls in hot oil in small batches, shaking the skillet back and forth to keep them moving so that they'll brown evenly. As they become golden, remove them to a dish lined with paper towels to absorb the excess oil.
9. Move the fried rice balls to a serving bowl and bring to the table. Fill each person's bowl with hot, steaming broth and drop 6-7 rice balls at a time into it. People will keep replenishing the rice balls as they eat. In this way the rice balls will remain nice and crisp in the broth. If you put too many into the broth at once, they'll become mushy and fall apart.
10. Serve with grated parmigiano and freshly ground black pepper.

SUGGESTED WINES:
Lacryma Christi del Vesuvio DOC bianco (Campania)

PAPPARDELLE ALLA BOSCAIOLA
Wide Noodles, Woodsman's Style

Pappardelle (wide egg noodles), see recipe on page 77	1 lb/500 gr
Fresh porcini mushrooms	10 ½ oz/300 gr
Dried porcini mushrooms	¼ cup/1 ¾ oz/50 gr
Ripe tomato, peeled and deprived of their seeds	7 oz/200 gr, chopped
Dry white wine	½ cup/100 cc
Rosemary	1 sprig fresh or 1 teaspoon dried
Extra virgin olive oil	¼ cup/50 cc
Salt	to taste
Hot chili pepper	to taste
Garlic	2 cloves
Grated parmigiano or pecorino	½ cup/100 gr

1. Prepare the pasta dough according to the recipe on page 77.
2. Divide the dough in 4 loaves. Using a rolling pin, roll each loaf out into a very thin sheet. Dust well with flour, then gently roll the sheets up.
3. Cut the pasta rolls into pappardelle about 1/2″/1 cm wide.
4. Heat the e.v.o.o. in a large skillet and introduce the dried porcini mushrooms, which have been previously soaked in tepid water for 30 minutes, drained, squeezed dry and and finely chopped.
5. Add the thinly sliced fresh mushrooms and cook over high heat.
6. Add the finely chopped hot chili pepper, salt, rosemary and the wine. Cook, stirring, to reduce the wine.
7. As all the flavors combine nicely, add the tomato and cook, uncovered, over medium-high heat for about 15 minutes, stirring frequently to keep the sauce from sticking to the pan.
8. Boil the pappardelle in abundant salted water. Remove and drain when quite al dente, and add to the sauce to cook for a few more minutes, tossing constantly.
9. Serve with the freshly grated cheese of your choice.

SUGGESTED WINES:
Lacryma Cristi del Vesuvio DOC Bianco - Campania

PASTA AL FORNO DI GIANNINA
Giannina's Baked Ziti

From the recipe of Giovanna Alfani Lonigo

Ziti	1 lb/500 gr
Tomato sauce or ragù, see recipes on page 81 and 84	1 qt/1 lt
Little meatballs, see recipe on page 83	10 ½ oz/300 gr
Eggs	4, hard boiled, sliced
Fresh mozzarella	7 oz/200 gr
Salami	3 ½ oz/100 gr, diced
Freshly grated parmigiano cheese	½ cup/100 gr

1. Cook the pasta in abundant salted water. When it's quite al dente, drain and dress with half of the tomato sauce or ragù.
2. Arrange a little over half of the pasta in a baking dish.
3. Spread a few spoonsful of sauce over this layer of pasta.
4. Distribute the slices of mozzarella, meatballs, salami and egg.
5. Sprinkle with grated parmigiano.
6. Spread a few spoonsful of sauce over all.
7. Distribute the rest of the ziti over the filling, packing it all in snugly.
8. Spread a few more spoonsful of sauce over the pasta and a generous sprinkle of grated parmigiano.
9. Bake at 350°F/180°C/Gas Mark 4 for 45 minutes.
10. Remove from the oven and allow to rest for 15-20 minutes before serving.

SUGGESTED WINES:
Aglianico del Taburno Rosso DOCG - Campania

PASTA ALLA SICILIANA
Baked Ziti Sicilian Style

Ziti	1 lb/500 gr
Long Italian eggplants	1 lb/500 gr
All purpose flour	1 cup/200 gr
Eggs	3, beaten
Tomato sauce or ragù, see recipe on page 81 or 84	2 qt/2 lt
Little meatballs, see recipe on page XXX	10 ½ oz/300 gr
Fresh mozzarella	7 oz/200 gr
Hard boiled eggs	4
Extra virgin olive oil	2 ⅓ cups/500 cc
Freshly ground black pepper	to taste
Freshly ground parmigiano	½ cup/100 gr

1. Slice the eggplants lengthwise about 1/4"/½ cm thick. Warm them in a non-stick pan to evaporate their liquid, then dust them in the flour, dredge them in the egg and fry in the olive oil.
2. As they become golden, lay them on paper towels to absorb any excess oil.
3. Cook the ziti in abundant salted water. When they are quite al dente, drain them and dress them generously with the tomato sauce or ragù
4. Distribute a little over half of the ziti in a baking dish.
5. Spoon some sauce evenly over the pasta.
6. Arrange the fried eggplant over the pasta, then spoon a little more sauce over it.
7. Distribute the sliced mozzarella, the meatballs and the sliced hard boiled egg over the eggplant.
8. Sprinkle with grated parmigiano, fresh ground pepper and a little more sauce.
9. Cover with the rest of the ziti, packing it all in snuggly.
10. Cover the top with more sauce, a generous dusting of grated parmigiano and freshly ground pepper.
11. Bake at 350°F/180°C/Gas Mark 4 for 45 minutes.
12. Remove from the oven and let rest for 15-20 minutes before serving.

SUGGESTED WINES:
Nero d'Avola - Sicilia

PASTA CON CARCIOFI E LIMONE
Pasta with Artichokes and Lemon

Linguine or penne pasta	1 lb / 500 gr
Artichokes	8, only the most tender parts and thinly sliced
Pinoli (pine nuts)	½ cup / 100 gr, pan roasted
Garlic	2 cloves, chopped
Oregano	2 or 3 sprigs fresh or 1 tablespoon dry
Zest of two organic lemons	
Extra virging olive oil	¼ cup / 50 cc
Salt and pepper	to taste
Grated parmigiano	¼ cup / 50 oz

1. Sauté the artichokes, garlic and salt in the e.v.o.o.
2. After 5 minutes, cover and cook over low flame for 15 minutes.
3. Uncover, add the oregano, pine nuts and lemon zest.
4. While the sauce is cooking, boil the pasta in abundant salted water. Drain when quite al dente and add to the sauce.
5. Toss the pasta with the sauce and sauté over medium heat for a few minutes.
6. Serve with parmigiano and freshly ground black pepper.

SUGGESTED WINES:
It's best to drink water with artichokes!

PASTA CON LE MELANZANE
Pasta with Eggplants

Penne, Calamarata or Ziti	1 lb / 500 gr
Eggplants	2 ¼ lb / 1 kg, cut into 1/2″ / 1 cm cubes
Grated parmigiano	½ cup / 100 gr
Diced tomatoes, deprived of their seeds	1 lb / 500 gr
Garlic	1 clove, chopped
Fresh basil	1 tablespoons, chopped
Extra virgin olive oil	as needed
Salt and pepper	to taste

1. Warm the cubed eggplants in a non-stick pan, with no oil, over a low flame to allow it to lose their liquid.
2. Fry the eggplant in the e.v.o.o. and remove them to dish covered with paper towels to absorb the excess oil.
3. Sauté the garlic in the e.v.o.o., add the tomatoes and salt and cook for 15 minutes.
4. Mix in the eggplant and chopped basil and sauté together for a few minutes to marry the flavors.
5. While the sauce was cooking, the pasta will have boiled in abundant salted water. Drain when it's quite al dente and toss into the sauce. Sauté together for 5 minutes.
6. Serve with grated parmigiano and freshly ground black pepper.

SUGGESTED WINES:

Etna Bianco DOC - Sicilia
Menfi Rosso DOC - Sicilia

PASTA E FAGIOLI CON LA ZUCCA
Pasta with white beans and pumpkin

In Tuscany, white cannellini beans have always been a staple.
In fact, they are so popular, the Tuscans earned themselves
the traditional nickname, "bean eaters"!
Here, our dish is sweetened with the addition of fresh pumpkin or butternut squash.

Mixed medium size pasta of your choice	1 lb/500 gr
White Cannellini Beans	1 ¼ cup/9 oz/250 gr
Pumpkin or butternut squash	1 lb/500 gr, diced
Hot chili pepper	to taste
Rosemary, sage and bay leaves	tied together into a bouquet
Extra virgin olive oil	½ cup/100 cc
Onion	1 large
Garlic	3 cloves
Tomato paste	2 tablespoons
White wine	½ cup/100 cc
White wine vinegar	1 tablespoon
Grated parmigiano	to taste

1. Soak the beans overnight.
2. Boil the beans for one hour in their own water.
3. Sauté the onion, garlic and chili pepper, all finely sliced, in the e.v.o.o.
4. Add the drained beans.
5. Stir and cook for 15 minutes. Using a fork, mash ⅓ of the beans.
6. Add the herbs and the tomato paste dissolved in the wine.
7. Stir well, add the pumpkin or squash
8. Add the diced pumpkin or squash.
9. Stir in the raw pasta. We like to use mixed pasta - all the little bits that seem to collect in the cupboard that are not enough to make one portion but too much to throw away. Mixed pasta lends itself to this dish - so much so that it's now sold in the stores, and it has a name: "minuzzaglia"!
10. Add enough hot water to cover the pasta. Cook, stirring frequently and adding boiling water if necessary.
11. When the pasta is cooked al dente, turn off the heat, cover and allow it to rest for 10-15 minutes before serving. The dish should remain moist, not dry.
12. Serve with our without grated parmigiano.

SUGGESTED WINES:
Gioia del Colle Rosato DOC - Puglia

PASTA E PATATE
Pasta with Potatoes

Mixed pasta	10 oz/300 gr
Potatoes	1 lb/500 gr, cut into 1/2"/1 cm cubes
Carrots	2 small, diced
Onion	1 large, chopped
Celery	1 small stalk, chopped
Garlic	2 cloves, chopped
Tomato paste	2 tablespoons
Dry white wine	¾ cup/150 cc
Extra virgin olive oil	½ cup/100 gr
Fresh flat leaf parsley	1 tablespoon, chopped
Grated parmigiano	½ cup/100 gr
Salt and pepper	to taste

1. Slowly sautè the carrots, celery and onions in the e.v.o.o. over medium heat for 10 minutes. Add the chopped garlic.
2. When the garlic becomes golden, add the tomato paste dissolved in the wine.
3. When the wine has reduced, add the potatoes and mix in well. Add 2-3 glasses of water and bring to a boil. When the water boils, mix in the raw pasta, salt and pepper.
4. Cook the pasta, stirring frequently to be sure that it doesn't stick to the bottom of the saucepan, adding hot water if necessary.
5. When the pasta is al dente and not too dry, turn off the flame.
6. Mix in the parsley and let rest, covered for 10 minutes.
7. Serve with grated parmigiano and freshly ground black pepper.

SUGGESTED WINES:
Gioia del Colle Rosato DOC - Puglia

PASTA GRATINATA AL TONNO
Pasta Gratin with Tuna

Smooth penne pasta	1 lb/500 gr
Tuna in olive oil	10 oz/300 gr
Extra virgin olive oil	2 tablespoons
White onions	4 medium, thinly sliced
Garlic	1 clove, finely chopped
Curry powder	a pinch
All purpose flour	1 tablespoon
Milk	1 ¼ cup/250 cc, warmed
Fresh flat leaf parsely	2 tablespoons, chopped
Breadcrumbs	¼ cup/50 gr
Grated parmigiano	½ cup/100 gr
Butter	3 ½ tablespoons/50 gr
Salt and pepper	to taste

1. Sautè the onion and garlic in the e.v.o.o.
2. When the onion is transparent and begins to turn golden, add the tuna and the curry.
3. Crumble the tuna well with a fork, stir well and sauté for 10 minutes.
4. Add the flour and slowly pour the milk in, stirring constantly.
5. Keep stirring as the sauce thickens.
6. Add the parsley, pepper and half the parmigiano.
7. While the sauce has been cooking, the pasta has been boiling in abundant salted water. When quite al dente, drain well and mix into the sauce.
8. Put the dressed pasta into a ring pan that has been greased and dusted with breadcrumbs. Dust the surface of the pasta with the remaining breadcrumbs and parmigiano, lots of freshly ground black pepper and dots of butter.
9. Bake at 350°F/180°C Gas Mark 4 for 30 minutes.

SUGGESTED WINES:
Ischia Biancolella DOC (white) - Campania

PENNE AI QUATTRO FORMAGGI
Penne with Four Cheeses

Smooth penne pasta	14 oz / 400 gr
Fresh mozzarella	3 ½ oz / 100 gr, in small cubes
Fontina	3 ½ oz / 100 gr, in small cubes
Gorgonzola	3 ½ oz / 100 gr, in small cubes
Grated parmigiano	½ cup / 100 gr
Milk	¼ cup / 50 cc
Freshly ground black pepper	1 teaspoon
Butter	3 ½ tablespoons / 50 gr
Breadcrumbs	¼ cup / 50 gr

1. Cook the pasta in abundant salted water. As the pasta cooks, prepare the sauce:
2. Boil the milk with the pepper in a saucepan for a couple of minutes.
3. Add the mozzarella, fontina, gorgonzola and half the parmigiano to the milk.
4. When the pasta is quite al dente, drain well and add to the sauce. Mix very well, stirring quickly.
5. Put the dressed pasta into a baking dish that has been greased and dusted with the breadcrumbs. Dust the surface of the pasta with breadcrumbs, the other half of the parmigiano, salt and pepper and dots of butter.
6. Bake at 400°F / 200°C / Gas Mark 6 for 30 minutes.

SUGGESTED WINES:
Verdicchio di Matelica DOC (white) - Marche
Terre di Franciacorta DOC (white) - Puglia

PENNE AI PEPERONI
Penne with Sweet Peppers

Penne pasta	1 lb/500 gr
Sweet red bell peppers	2 lb/1 kg
Extra virgin olive oil	¼ cup/50 gr
Garlic	3 cloves, crushed
Mascarpone	3 tablespoons
Fresh basil leaves	2 tablespoons, chopped and several whole leaves
Salt	to taste

1. Roast the peppers for 30 minutes in the oven at 400°F/200°C/Gas Mark 6
2. Peel the roasted peppers, clean them of their seeds and chop all but one of them. Cut the last pepper in 16 thin slices.
3. Warm the oil in a saucepan with the garlic. When the garlic becomes golden, remove it.
4. Lightly sautè the 16 pepper strips in the garlic-infused oil, remove and set aside.
5. In the same oil, sauté the chopped peppers, add salt to taste. Cook for a few minutes over medium flame. As they cook, they'll begin to dissolve into a purée.
6. Add the basil and the mascarpone.
7. Add the pasta which has been boiled in abundant salted water until al dente and drained. Sauté with the sauce for a few minutes.
8. Serve the pasta decorated with 4 pepper slices and 3 basil leaves.

SUGGESTED WINES:
Lamezia Greco DOC (white) - Calabria

PENNE ALLA CARBONARA

*"Carbone" in Italian means charcoal. Penne alla carbonara is liberally
dusted with freshly ground black pepper before serving, hence he name.*

Penne pasta	1 lb/500 gr
Pancetta	5 oz/150 gr, finely diced
Eggs	4, beaten
Extra virgin olive oil	¼ cup/50 cc
Grated parmigiano	1 cup/100 gr
Salt and pepper	to taste

1. Slowly cook the pancetta in a pan with the e.v.o.o. over low heat until all its fat
   has rendered.
2. Cook the pasta in abundant salted water and drain when quite al dente. Add to
   the the pancetta and cook over high flame, tossing vigorously, for a minute or two.
3. Turn off the heat. Mix in the parmigiano and pepper.
4. Pour the beaten eggs over the pasta and mix vigorously.
5. Serve the pasta in warmed dishes, dusted generously with parmigiano and freshly ground black pepper.

SUGGESTED WINES:
Frascati Superiore DOC (white) - Lazio

PENNE ALLA MAREMMANA

Maremma is the coastal area of southern Tuscany where even today,
"i butteri", Tuscan cowboys, ride the range.
This is a dish we learned to love when we lived there in the early 1980's

Smooth penne pasta	1 lb/500 gr
Onion	1, sliced
Garlic	2 cloves, chopped
Baked black olives	1 cup/100 gr, pitted
Fresh flat leaf parsley	1 tablespoon, chopped
Hot chili pepper	to taste
Diced tomatoes	½ lb/250 gr
Mascarpone	2-3 tablespoons
Extra virgin olive oil	as needed
Salt	to taste
Freshly grated pecorino cheese	½ cup/100 gr

1. Sautè the onion and the garlic in the e.v.o.o., add the chili peppers
2. Add the tomato and olives. Sautè over medium heat but don't allow to dry too much!
3. Boil the pasta in abudant salted water. Drain when al dente and add to the sauce.
4. Mix well, adding the mascarpone and parsley.
5. Serve with freshly grated pecorino.

SUGGESTED WINES:
Morellino di Scansano DOCG (red) - Toscana

PICI CON PORCINI
Pici with Porcini Mushrooms

Pici are typical hand-rolled long pasta from Tuscany.
You can also use spaghetti or tagliatelle

Pici or similar long pasta	1 lb / 500 gr
Fresh porcini mushrooms	1 lb / 500 gr sliced
Dried porcini mushrooms	¼ cup / 50 gr
Dry white wine	½ cup / 100 cc
Tomato paste	1 tablespoon
Garlic	2 cloves, thinly sliced
Fresh flat leaf parsely	2 tablespoons
Extra virgin olive oil	2 tablespoons
Salt	to taste
Hot chili pepper	to taste
Freshly grated parmigiano or pecorino	½ cup / 100 gr

1. While you prepare the sauce, boil the pici in abundant salted water and drain when quite al dente.
2. Sautè the garic in the e.v.o.o.
3. Add the dried porcini, previously soaked in warm water until tender, drained and squeezed dry, then finely chopped.
4. Add the chili peppers.
5. Add the fresh porcini mushrooms and sautè over medium-high heat until they give up their liquids. When they are about halfway cooked, add the tomato paste which will have been dissolved in the wine. Continue cooking until the liquids have reduced.
6. Add the cooked, drained pici to the sauce and sautè for a 5 minutes over high heat.
7. Serve steaming hot with grated pecorino cheese.

SUGGESTED WINES:
Pomino DOC (red) - Toscana

PICI FOSSA E PEPE
Pici, Formaggio di Fossa and Black Pepper

*Formaggio di fossa is an ancient cheese from the mountainous regions where
Le Marche, Tuscany and Emlia-Romagna meet. The cheese, made of sheep's milk or sheep's
milk mixed with cow's milk, is wrapped in burlap, covered with straw,
then aged for three months in stone pits.*

Pici or similar long pasta	1 lb/500 gr
Formaggio di fossa	3 ½ oz/100 gr, coarsely grated and 1 ¾ oz/50 gr, thin shavings
Coarsely ground black pepper	2 tablespoons
Heavy cream	½ cup/100 cc
Juniper berries	1 tablespoon
Salt	to taste

1. Cook the pici in abundant salted water. When al dente, add them to a pan containing the heavy cream, juniper berries, half of the ground pepper and grated formaggio di fossa.
2. Mix well and sauté for a few minutes until the cheese has melted and the sauce thickened. Serve topped with the cheese shavings and more black pepper.

SUGGESTED WINES:
Elba Bianco DOC - Toscana
Chianti Classico DOCG - Toscana

RAVIOLI ALLE MELANZANE
Eggplant Ravioli

Fresh egg pasta in sheets, see recipe on page 77	1 lb/500 gr
Tomato sauce, see recipe on page 81	1 qt/1 lt
Eggplants	2 large
Fresh flat leaf parsley	2 tablespoons, chopped
Eggs	2
Garlic	1 clove
Extra virgin olive oil	3 tablespoons
Salt and pepper	to taste
Grated parmigiano	4 tablespoons plus ⅓ cup/100 gr
Butter	½ cup/100 gr

1. Bake the eggplants, whole, at 350°F/400°C/Gas Mark 6 for one hour.
2. Remove from the oven. When they have cooled, remove the skins and cut the pulp into small pieces.
3. Brown the garlic in the e.v.o.o., remove when it's nicely golden.
4. Add the eggplant pulp to the pan and cook, stirring contantly, allowing them to release and reduce their liquids, then finely chop them.
5. Remove from the heat and allow to cool. Add the parsley, 1 tablespoon of parmigiano and the eggs. Mix everything until smoothly blended.
6. Roll the pasta out into two thin sheets.
7. If the mixture is too moist, add more parmigiano.
8. Roll the dough out into two thin sheets. Place little balls of eggplant filling, about the size of a hazelnut, at regular distances on one of the sheets. Cover with the other sheet, then using a ravioli-cutter or an upturned glass of the proper size, press down on each raviolo to cut through the two sheets of pasta. If you use a glass instead of the ravioli tool, you'll have to seal each raviolo by pressing down the edges with the tines of a fork.
9. Cook the ravioli in abundant boiling water. When they are cooked, use a slotted spoon or skimmer to remove them to a large serving dish.
10. Dress the ravioli with tomato sauce.
11. Serve with grated parmigiano.

SUGGESTED WINES:
Vermentino di Gallura DOCG (white) - Sardegna

RAVIOLI AL FORNO
Baked Ravioli

Fresh egg pasta in sheets, see recipe on page 77	1 lb/500 gr
omato sauce, see recipe on page 81	1 qt/1 lt
Lean ground beef	5 ½ oz/150 gr
Lean ground pork	5 ½ oz/150 gr
Ground prosciutto	3 ½ oz/100 gr
Eggs	2
Dry white wine	½ cup/100 cc
Grated parmigiano	⅓ cup/80 gr
Onion	1 small, thinly sliced
Garlic	1 clove, finely chopped
Extra virgin olive oil	¼ cup/50 cc
Tomato paste	2 tablespoons
Salt and pepper	to taste

1. Sauté the onion and garlic in the e.v.o.o. When they begin to turn golden, add the tomato paste which will have been dissolved in the wine. Mix in the meats, crumbling them with a fork.
2. When the meats have browned, remove to a mixing bowl and allow to cool. Mix in the eggs, parmigiano, salt and pepper.
3. Refrigerate for one hour.
4. Roll out two thin sheets of pasta.
5. On one of the sheets, arrange little balls of filling, about the size of a hazelnut, at regular distances.
6. Cover with the other sheet of pasta and, using a ravioli-cutting tool or an upturned glass of the desired size, cut out each raviolo. If you use a glass to cut out the ravioli, you'll have to seal the edges by pressing down on them with the tines of a fork.
7. Cook the ravioli in abundant boiling salted water. When they're quite al dente, use a slotted spoon or skimmer to remove them to a large mixing bowl.
8. Dress the ravioli with tomato sauce.
9. Place the ravioli in a baking dish, cover with more sauce, sprinkle with parmigiano and black pepper and bake at 400°F/200°C/Gas Mark 6 for 30 minutes.
10. Remove from the oven and allow to rest for 15 minutes before serving.
11. To serve, cut into slices as you would do with lasagne.

SUGGESTED WINES:
Taburno Rosso DOC - Campania

RAVIOLI CON FAGIOLI
Ravioli with Beans

Fresh egg pasta in sheets, see recipe on page 77	1 lb/500 gr
White cannellini beans	7 oz/200 gr
Tomato paste	1 tablespoon
Dry white wine	¼ cup/50 cc
Fresh flat leaf parsley	2 tablespoons, chopped
Eggs	2
Garlic	one clove, chopped
Extra virgin olive oil	3 tablespoons
Salt and pepper	to taste
Grated parmigiano	½ oz/100 gr
Butter	½ cup/100 gr
Fresh sage	1 tablespoon, thinly sliced

1. Soak the beans for 12 hours in cool water.
2. Cook the beans in their water for one hour.
3. Sauté the garlic in the e.v.o.o. Add the tomato paste which has been dissolved in the wine. then the cooked drained beans.
4. Cook over medium heat to allow the flavors to marry. Use a fork to mash some of the beans as they cook - this will thicken the sauce.
5. Remove from the heat. When the beans have cooled, mix in the parsley, a tablespoon of parmigiano, salt and pepper and the eggs. If the filling is too thin, it can be thicken with the addition of a little more grated parmigiano.
6. Roll out two thin sheets of pasta.
7. On one of the sheets, arrange little balls of filling, about the size of a hazelnut, at regular distances. Cover with the other sheet of pasta and, using a ravioli-cutting tool or an upturned glass of the desired size, cut out each raviolo. If you use a glass to cut out the ravioli, you'll have to seal the edges by pressing down on them with the tines of a fork.
8. Cook the ravioli in abundant boiling salted water. When they're quite al dente, use a slotted spoon or skimmer to remove them to a large seving bowl.
9. Dress the ravioli with the butter which has been melted and infused with the sage.
10. Serve with grated parmigiano and freshly ground black pepper.

SUGGESTED WINES:
Velletri Bianco DOC - Lazio

RISI E BISI

A typical dish from the Veneto region, it is somewhere in between
a risotto and a rice soup with peas! The recipe was brought into the family by
a great friend, Renzo Braggio, who was from Verona, where the saying goes,
"Ogni riso, un biso" - to each grain of rice, its pea!

Arborio rice	1 lb / 500 gr
Tender tiny peas	1 lb / 500 gr
Spring onions or scallions	4, very finely chopped
Dry white wine	½ cup / 100 cc
Extra virgin olive oil	¼ cup / 50 gr
Pancetta	3 ½ oz / 100 gr, diced
Butter	1 ¾ oz / 50 gr
Vegetable broth	1 ¼ cup / 250 cc
Grated parmigiano	¼ cup / 50 gr
Salt and pepper	to taste

1. Cook the rice in abundant boiling salted water. Drain when al dente and set aside.
2. In a saucepan, sautè the pancetta in the butter and oil over medium-low heat to render the pancetta's fat. Add the onions.
3. When the onions turn transparent, add the peas, mixing thoroughly so that their flavors marry.
4. Cover the peas with water and cook until tender.
5. Let the water reduce, then add the rice, stirring and mixing it thoroughly to infuse it with the flavors. Add the broth and cook 5 minutes over high heat, stirring, until it becomes creamy. At this point, add salt, pepper and the grated parmigiano.
6. Mix well and serve hot.

- This dish is best when fresh peas are in season.

SUGGESTED WINES:
Tocai DOC (white) - Veneto

RISO E FAGIOLI DI JUANA
Rice and beans (Juana's Arroz con Frijoles)

*From the recipe of Juana Matilla Martinez, Eugene's mother.
The addition of a spoonful of vinegar when cooking beans was her secret
weapon against the "airy" problem that beans so often cause!*

Borlotti or kidney beans	1 lb / 500 gr
Yellow onion	1 large, sliced
Red bell pepper	1 small, chopped
Green bell pepper	1 small, chopped
Garlic	3-4 cloves, chopped
Peeled Roma tomatoes	14 oz / 400 gr
Powdered cumin	1 level teaspoon
Oregano	a pinch
Bay leaves	5 or 6
Red wine vinegar	1 tablespoon
Fresh flat leaf parsley	2 tablespoons, chopped
Salt and pepper	to taste
Olive oil	as needed
Thaibonnet rice	7 oz / 200 gr

1. Soak the beans overnight, at least 12 hours, in cool water. Drain, rinse under cold water then cook in abundant lightly salted water for one hour or until tender.
2. Sautè the onion in e.v.o.o. When the onion becomes transparent, add the garlic and peppers.
3. When the peppers are cooked yet still have a little crunch, add the peeled tomatoes, crushing them with your hands, along with some of their liquid.
4. Add the cumin, bay leaves, salt and pepper.
5. Cook for a few minutes to marry all the flavors, then add the drained beans and the vinegar. Continue cooking for 15-20 minutes over medium heat with the saucepan semi-covered.
6. In the meantime, cook the rice in lightly salted water.

- Serve the beans on a bed of rice, accompanied by Tabasco or the hot sauce of your choice and a 'pico de gallo' of papaya and scallion, fried ripe 'platanos' (plantains) and boiled yucca marinated in olive oil and lemon juice with cumin, and a salad of avocado and fresh green onions dressed with e.v.o.o. and lemon juice.

SUGGESTED WINES:
With arroz con frijoles, the beverage of choice is an ice cold blond beer.

RISOTTO CON I FIORI DI ZUCCA
Risotto with zucchini flowers

Originario rice	1lb/500gr
Vegetable broth, see recipe on page 67	2qt/2 lt
Fresh zucchini flowers	40 chopped and 8 whole
Onion, chopped	1 large
Extra virgin olive oil	¼ cup/50cc
Butter	¼ cup/50gr
Freshly grated parmigiano cheese	½ cup/100gr
Salt and pepper	to taste

1. Sautè the chopped onion in the e.v.o.o. with ⅔ of the butter.
2. Add the chopped zucchini flowers and sautè for a minute or two.
3. Add the whole zucchini flowers and sautè only long enough to flavor them with the onion, then remove and set aside.
4. Add the rice and "toast" it for 10 minutes. By toasting, we mean sautè it, stirring often, until its outer surface achieves a beautiful gloss.
5. Add the hot broth, one ladleful at a time and stir constantly. As the broth is absorbed, add more.
6. Add the salt and continue cooking until the rice is slightly al dente.
7. Remove from the heat and stir in the rest of the butter, half of the parmigiano and pepper to taste.
8. Allow the risotto to rest for 10 minutes uncovered.
9. Garnish each dish with one whole cooked zucchini flower.
10. Serve with parmigiano and freshly ground black pepper.

SUGGESTED WINES:
Velletri Bianco DOC - Lazio

RISO E PATATE
Rice with Potatoes

Rice	10 ½ oz / 300 gr
Potatoes	1 lb / 500 gr, diced
Fresh flat leaf parsley	1 tablespoon, chopped
Celery	1 stalk, chopped
Onion	1 large, chopped
Carrots	2 small, chopped
Garlic	1 clove, chopped
Extra virgin olive oil	¼ cup / 50 cc
Dry white wine	¼ cup / 50 cc
Tomato paste	1 tablespoon
Salt and pepper	to taste
Grated parmigiano	as you like

1. Cook the rice in abundant lightly salted water. While the rice is cooking, prepare the following:
2. Sautè the onions and garlic in the e.v.o.o. Add the carrots and celery and continue to sauté over medium-low heat.
3. Add the tomato paste which has been dissolved in the wine.
4. Add the potatoes with 2 glasses of water. Cover and cook 20 minutes.
5. Uncover, raise the heat and reduce the liquids.
6. Drain the rice when it is quite al dente. Mix well and cook for a few minutes, stirring constantly, until it becomes creamy.
7. Serve with grated parmigiano and freshly ground black pepper.

SUGGESTED WINES:
Lamezio Greco DOC (white) - Calabria

RISOTTO NAPOLETANO
Neopolitan Risotto

Arborio or Vialone rice	1 lb/500 gr
Meat broth, see recipe on page 67	2 qt/2 lt
Onion	1 large, chopped
Lean pancetta	3 ½ oz/100 gr, diced
Garlic	2 cloves, chopped
Extra virgin olive oil	¼ cup/50 cc
Grated parmigiano	½ cup/100 gr
Fresh flat leaf parsley	1 tablespoon, chopped
Tomato paste	3 ½ oz/100 gr
Dry white wine	1 cup/200 cc
Salt and pepper	to taste

1. Sauté the onion, garlic and pancetta in the e.v.o.o.
2. Add the tomato paste which has been diluted in the wine.
3. Add the rice, stirring well to mingle the flavors. Continue to cook, stirring, for 5-6 minutes.
4. Begin to add the hot broth one ladle at a time, and stirring continuously over a medium flame, let the rice absorb the liquids. As the broth is absobed, add another ladleful, stirring. Keep adding the broth one ladleful at a time until the rice is al dente yet creamy and smooth.
5. Remove from the heat, adjust salt and pepper, mix in the parmigiano and chopped parsley.
6. Allow to rest for 10 minutes before serving.

- This risotto is ideal to prepare Sartù di Riso, see recipe on page 154.

SUGGESTED WINES:
Vesuvio Rosso DOC - Campania

RISOTTO AI PORCINI
Risotto with Porcini Mushrooms

Arborio rice	1 lb / 500 gr
Meat broth, see recipe on page 67	2 qt / 2 lt
Dry porcini mushrooms	¼ cup / 50 gr, soaked, squeezed dry and finely chopped
Fresh porcini or other mushrooms	10 ½ oz / 300 gr, sliced
Extra virgin olive oil	¼ cup / 50 cc
Butter	3 ½ oz / 100 gr
Garlic	2 cloves, chopped
Onion	1 large
Tomato paste	2 tablespoons
Dry white wine	½ cup / 100 cc
Grated parmigiano	3 ½ oz / 100 gr
Fresh flat leaf parsley	2 tablespoon, chopped
Salt and pepper	to taste

1. Sauté the onion and garlic in the e.v.o.o. and half the butter.
2. Add the dried mushrooms, sauté for a minute or two.
3. Add the fresh mushrooms, and cook for about 20 minutes, stirring frequently.
4. Add the tomato paste which has been dissolved in the wine, salt and pepper.
5. Add the rice and toast it in this sauce, stirring contantly, for about 10 minutes. The external surface of each kernel will become glossy and slick.
6. Begin to add the hot broth, one ladleful at a time, stirring constantly. As the broth is absorbed by the rice, add more. Continue to stir and add broth until the rice is cooked al dente and has become creamy and smooth.
7. Remove the risotto from the heat and blend in the remaining butter, half of the parmigiano and the parsley.
8. Allow to rest for 5 minutes. Stir once, serve with more grated parmigiano.

SUGGESTED WINES:
Cori Rosso DOC - Lazio

RISO AI PORRI E GAMBERONI
Rice with Leeks and Prawns

Vegetable broth, see recipe on page 67	2 qt / 2 lt
Rice	10 ½ oz / 300 gr
Leeks	1 lb / 500 gr, chopped
Prawns or jumbo shrimps with the tail	8
Extra virgin olive oil	¼ cup / 50 cc
Butter	¼ / 50 gr
Salt and pepper	to taste

1. Toast the rice in the butter and half the e.v.o.o. for 5-6 minutes.
2. When the rice becomes glossy, add vegetable broth to cover and continue cooking, stirring, until the rice is cooked al dente and the broth has been absorbed.
3. Remove from heat and allow to rest for 5 minutes. Meanwhile, line four molds or cups with transparent cling wrap.
4. Fill each mold with rice, packing firmly. Turn each mold over onto its own plate. Delicately remove the rice from the mold, peeling away the cling wrap.
5. In a small pan, sauté the leeks in the other half of the e.v.o.o. and butter. Add the prawns which have been peeled but which have kept their tails.
6. Sauté for 5 minutes
7. Spoon the leeks and two prawns over each portion of rice.

SUGGESTED WINES:
Sannio Falanghina DOC (white) - Campania

RISOTTO ALLO ZAFFERANO
Risotto with Saffron

Rice	10 ½ oz/300 gr
Meat broth, see recipe on page 67	1 ½ qt/1 ½ lt
Saffron	½ teaspoon/1 gr, steeped in a jigger of warm broth
Butter	½ cup/100 gr
Extra virgin olive oil	¼ cup/50 cc
Onions	3, finely chopped
Salt and pepper	to taste
Grated parmigiano	½ cup/100 gr

1. Sauté the onion in the e.v.o.o. and half the butter.
2. Add the rice and let it toast for 5 minutes, stirring constantly.
3. Add one ladleful of hot broth. Stir, add the saffron with its broth.
4. Continue cooking, adding one ladleful of hot broth at a time, stirring constantly. As the rice absorbs the broth, add more until the rice is al dente and has attained a smooth, creamy consistancy.
5. Remove from the heat. Blend in the rest of the butter, the black pepper and half the parmigiano.
6. Mix well, allow to rest for 5 minutes.
7. Serve with more parmigiano and black pepper.

SUGGESTED WINES:
Parrina Rosato DOC - Toscana

RISOTTO ZUCCA E PISELLI
Risotto with Pumpkin and Peas

Arborio rice	1 lb/500 gr
Vegetable broth, see recipe on page 67	2 qt/2 lt
Extra virgin olive oil	¼ cup/50 cc
Butter	¼ cup/60 gr
Shallots	4, chopped
Peas	7 oz/200 gr
Pumpkin or butternut squash	10 ½ oz/300 gr
Fresh flat leaf parsley	1 tablespoon, chopped
Grated parmigiano	½ cup/100 gr
Salt and pepper	to taste

1. Sauté the shallots in the e.v.o.o. Add the peas and the rice and stir, toasting the rice for about 5 miutes, until it's glossy.
2. Add the hot broth one ladleful at a time, stirring continuously. As the broth is absorbed by the rice, add another ladleful. Continue in this way until the rice is al dente and has achieved a creamy texture.
3. While the rice is cooking, sauté the pumpkin in a separate sauce pan with a little e.v.o.o. When it is al dente, mix it into the rice for its last 5 minutes of cooking.
4. Remove the risotto from the heat and blend in the butter, parsley and half the parmigiano.
5. Serve hot with more grated parmigiano on top.

SUGGESTED WINES:
Pàmpini Maroso (white) - Lazio

SARTÙ DI RISO

Among the most Neapolitan of Neapolitan dishes, you'll never find Sartù on a restaurant menu. This is a dish that is always prepared in the homes of Naples' most traditional families.

Carnaroli rice	1 lb / 500 gr
Meat ragù, see recipe on page 84	2 qt / 2 lt
Little meatballs, see recipe on page 83	
Mozzarella	7 oz / 200 gr
Green peas	1 lb / 500 gr
Scallions	2 or 3, finely chopped
Hard boiled eggs	4
Lean salami	3 ½ oz / 100 gr, cut into small pieces
Butter	¼ cup / 50 gr
Breadcrumbs	½ cup / 100 gr
Grated parmigiano	½ cup / 100 gr
Salt and pepper	to taste

1. Cook the rice in abundant salted water. Drain when the rice is al dente, letting it run under cold water to stop the cooking process.
2. Dress the rice with a third of the ragù.
3. Cook the peas with the scallions in a little e.v.o.o.
4. Mix half of the cooked peas with the rice.
5. Grease a ring pan and dust with breadcrumbs. Place half of the rice into the ring pan.
6. Arrange the mozzarella, the hard boiled eggs cut into pieces, the salami, the other half of the peas and the meatballs. Hold a few meatballs to the side to be used later to decorate the portions.
7. Spoon more ragù over the filling.
8. Spread the remaining rice over the filling, patting it all down firmly.
9. Sprinkle with the remaining breadcrumbs and parmigiano.
10. Bake at 350°F/180°C/Gas Mark 4 for 40 minutes.
11. Remove from the oven and allow to rest for about 30 minutes.
12. With a sharp unserrated knife, go around the outer and inner perimeter of the ring pan to loosen the sartù from it, then turn it over onto a capacious serving dish.
13. Cut the sartù into portions. Serve each portion with a spoonful of ragù and a few of the little meatballs to decorate.

- The Sartù di Riso can also be made in small individual molds.

SUGGESTED WINES:
Vesuvio Rosso DOC - Campania

SARTÙ DI RISO BIANCO
White Sartù

Arborio rice	1lb/500 gr
Vegetable broth (see recipe on page 67)	2 qt/2 lt
Extra virgin olive oil	¼ cup/50 cc
Butter	½ cup/50 gr
Onions	3-4, chopped
Dry white wine	½ cup/100 cc
Hard boiled eggs	4
Dried porcini mushrooms	¼ cup/1 ¾ oz/50 gr, soaked, drained and chopped
Green peas	7 oz/200 gr
Smoked mozzarella	7 oz/200 gr
Rich bèschamel (see recipe on page 66)	1 qt/1 lt
Grated parmigiano	½ cup/100 gr
Breadcrumbs	¼ cup/ 50 gr
Salt and pepper	to taste

1. Prepare a risotto, very al dente, using the vegetable broth.
2. Sauté the onion in the oil and butter. Add the reconstituted porcini mushrooms.
3. Add the peas. Sauté for a few mintues, then add the wine. Reduce.
4. Mix the risotto with half of the rich bèchamel.
5. Grease a baking dish with butter and sprinkle with breadcrumbs. Spread a layer of the rice in the bottom of the dish.
6. Arrange the smoked mozzarella, the mushrooms, peas and the sliced eggs.
7. Spoon more bèschamel over the filling, then cover with the rest of the rice.
8. Bake at 400°F/200°C/Gas Mark 6 for 40 minutes.
9. Remove from the oven and allow to rest for 15-20 minutes before serving.

SUGGESTED WINES:
Lacryma Christi del Vesuvio DOC (white) - Campania

SPAGHETTI ALLA PUTTANESCA

Spaghetti	1 lb/500 gr
Greek or Gaeta olives	¾ cup/150 gr, pitted and torn in half
Salted capers	¼ cup/50 gr, washed of their salt in tepid water and dried
Garlic	2 large cloves, sliced
Hot chili pepper	to taste
Oregano	a pinch
Peeled Roma tomatoes	7-14 oz/200-400 gr, depending on how red you like your sauce, diced
Extra virgin olive oil	as needed

1. Cook the spaghetti in abundant boiling salted water. Drain when al dente. While the pasta cooks, prepare the sauce:
2. Sauté all the ingredients but the tomatoes in enough e.v.o.o. to cover the bottom of a pan.
3. Add the tomatoes and oregano. Cook, mixing, over medium high heat for a few minutes. Toss the spaghetti in with the sauce and serve piping hot.

- A delicious way to use leftover spaghetti alla puttanesca is in a frittata!

SUGGESTED WINES:
Colli della Sabina DOC (red) - Lazio

SPAGHETTI CON LE VONGOLE
Spaghetti with Clams

Spaghetti	1 lb/500 gr
Manila or other very small clams	1 lb/500 gr, soaked and scrubbed
	Extra virgin olive oil - ¼ cup/50 cc
Dry white wine	¼ cup/50 cc
Garlic	3 cloves, thinly sliced
Ripe cherry tomatoes	7 oz/200 gr, cut in half
Fresh flat leaf parsley	2 tablespoons, chopped
Salt and pepper	to taste

1. Cook the spaghetti in abundant boiling salted water. Drain when al dente.
2. While the pasta cooks, prepare the sauce:
3. Put the clams in a large pan with no oil over medium heat. When the clams have opened, remove from the heat. Drain, filter and set aside the broth.
4. Remove 2/3 of the clams from their shells. Sautè all the clams in the e.v.o.o. with the garlic.
5. Add salt, pepper, the wine and the clam broth which will have been filtered through a fine sieve.
6. Cook, uncovered, over high heat for 5 minutes.
7. Toss with the spaghetti, mix in the chopped parsley and serve.

SUGGESTED WINES:
Verdicchio dei Castelli di Jesi Bianco DOC - Marche

SPAGHETTI E BROCCOLI DI RAPE
Spaghetti with Broccoli Rabe

Spaghetti	14 oz / 400 gr
Broccoli rabe	2 lb / 1 kg
Garlic	2 cloves, chopped
Hot chili pepper	to taste
Extra virgin olive oil	as needed
Salt	to taste

1. Clean the broccoli of all but its tenderest leaves and flowerettes.
2. Steam them lightly, then coarsely chop them.
3. Sauté the garlic in the e.v.o.o., add the chili pepper to taste.
4. Add the broccoli and stir-fry over medium-high heat, adding a little very hot water if necessary.
5. Cook the spaghetti in abundant boiling salted water. Drain when al dente.
6. Add to the broccoli and continue to cook together, tossing frequently, for another couple of minutes.
7. Serve piping hot.

SUGGESTED WINES:
Vermentino di Gallura DOCG (white) - Sardegna
Lacryma Christi del Vesuvio DOC (white) - Campania

TAGLIATELLE FUNGHI E PEPERONI
Tagliatelle with Mushrooms and Peppers

Egg tagliatelle, see recipe on page 77	14 oz / 400 gr
Dried porcini mushrooms	¼ cup / 50 gr
Fresh mushrooms	7 oz / 200 gr
Red bell peppers	2 large, cleaned of their seeds and cut into small pieces.
Onions	4, chopped
Garlic	2 cloves, thinily sliced
Dry white wine	2 teaspoons / 10 cc
Mascarpone	3 tablespoons
Extra virgin olive oil	¼ cup / 50 gr
Fresh flat leaf parsley	2 tablespoons, chopped
Salt and pepper	to taste

1. Soak the dry porcini in warm water until tender. Drain and squeeze them dry, then chop finely.
2. Thinly slice the fresh mushrooms.
3. Sauté the onions in the e.v.o.o. along with the garlic. Add the fresh mushrooms and the peppers, which have been cleaned of their seeds and chopped in pieces no larger than the mushroom slices. Add the salt, pepper and wine. Cook for 15 minutes uncovered, stirring frequently.
4. Remove from the heat. Blend in the parsley and the mascarpone.
5. While you've been preparing the sauce, the tagliatelle have been cooking in abundant boiling salted water. Drain them when al dente and toss them with the sauce.

SUGGESTED WINES:
Montecarlo Bianco DOC - Toscana
Castel del Monte DOC (white) - Puglia

TAGLIOLINI CON I GAMBERI
Tagliolini with Shrimp

Egg tagliolini, see recipe on page 77	14 oz / 400 gr
Small shrimp	10 ½ oz / 300 gr, peeled
Jumbo shrimp	8, peeled but with their tails
Garlic	2 cloves, finely chopped
Dry white wine	¼ cup / 50 cc
Fresh flat leaf parsley	2 tablespoons, chopped
Extra virgin olive oil	¼ cup / 50 cc
Zest of 1 organic lemon	
Salt and pepper	to taste

1. Sauté the garlic in the e.v.o.o. for a minute, then add all the shrimp. Add the wine, half the parsley and a squeeze of lemon juice. Cook for 3 minutes over high flame.
2. Remove the jumbo shrimp to a warm plate.
3. While you've been preparing the sauce, the tagliolini were cooking in abundant boiling salted water. Drain them al dente and toss with the shrimp sauce.
4. Serve the tagliolini, decorating each dish with 2 jumbo shrimps, parsley and a dusting of lemon zest.

SUGGESTED WINES:
Montefalco Bianco - Umbria

TAGLIOLINI DELLA NONNA
Grandmother's Tagliolini

Egg tagliolini, see recipe on page 77	14 oz / 400 gr
or tortellini or pappardelle	
Heavy cream	1 ¼ cup / 250 cc
Butter	¼ cup / 50 gr
Lean prosciutto	5 ½ oz / 250 gr, sliced julienne
Green peas	7 oz / 200 gr
White onions	2 small, thinly sliced
Grated parmigiano	½ cup / 100 gr
Salt and pepper	to taste

1. Sauté the onion in butter. Add the peas, salt and cover with hot water.
2. Cook, uncovered, for about 30 minutes, allowing the liquid to evaporate.
3. Warm the cream in a saucepan.
4. Introduce the prosciutto and cook in the cream for 5 minutes.
5. Add the cooked peas to the cream.
6. While you've been preparing the sauce, the tagliolini have been cooking in abundant boiling salted water. Drain when al dente and toss with the cream sauce along with the parmigiano and freshly ground black pepper.
7. Mix well and serve hot.

SUGGESTED WINES:
Trebbiano d'Abruzzo DOC (white) - Abruzzo

TAGLIOLINI GRATINATI DI ANGELICA
Angelica's Tagliolini Gratin

From the recipe of Angelica Alfani Latour

Egg tagliolini, see recipe on page 77	1 lb / 500 gr
Rich béschamel, see recipe on page 66	1 qt / 1 lt
Tender green peas	1 lb / 500 gr
Spring onions	5 small, finely sliced
Provola (smoked mozzarella)	10 ½ oz / 300 gr, in small cubes
Extra virgin olive oil	¼ cup / 50 cc
Butter	¼ cup / 50 gr
Grated parmigiano	½ cup / 100 gr
Breadcrumbs	½ / 100 gr
Salt and pepper to taste	

1. Sauté the onion in the butter and e.v.o.o.
2. Add the green peas, salt and pepper. Stir, pour in a glass of water and cook for 30 minutes until the water has evaporated.
3. Cook the tagliolini in abundant boiling salted water until al dente. Drain.
4. Pour half of the peas into the béchamel.
5. Dress the tagliolini with 3/4 of the béschamel.
6. Grease and dust a baking dish with breadcrumbs. Spread 2/3 of the tagliolini in the pan.
7. Arrange the rest of the peas and the provola over the tagliolini, then cover with the remaining pasta.
8. Spoon more béchamel over the surface of the pasta, sprinkle with grated parmigiano, breadcrumbs and dots of butter.
9. Bake at 400°F/200°C Gas Mark 6 for 30 minutes or until a nice golden crust has formed.
10. Remove from the oven and allow to rest for 15 minutes before serving.

- This recipe can be prepared in individual molds.

SUGGESTED WINES:
Lacryma Christi del Vesuvio DOC (white) - Campania

TAGLIOLINI GRATINATI ALLA GENOVESE
Baked Tagliolini Genovese

Egg tagliolini, see recipe on page 77	1 lb/500 gr
Genovese sauce, see recipe on page 70	1 qt/1 lt
Little meatballs, see recipe on page 83	300 gr
Grated parmigiano	¼ cup/50 gr
Fresh mozzarella	7 oz/200 gr, sliced
Green peas	7 oz/200 gr
Spring onions	2, thinly sliced
Extra virgin olive oil	2 tablespoons/25 cc
Butter	¼ cup/50 gr
Breadcrumbs	½/100 gr
Salt and pepper	to taste

1. Cook the onions in the e.v.o.o. and half the butter.
2. Add the peas, season with salt and pepper, pour in a glass of water and cook the peas for 30 minutes or until all the liquids have reduced.
3. Cook the tagliolini in abundant salted water. Drain when quite al dente and dress with 2/3 of the warm genovese sauce.
4. Grease a baking dish and dust it with breadcrumbs. Spread 2/3 of the dressed tagliolini in the pan, then cover it with the little meatballs, the peas and the sliced mozzarella over it. Spread a few spoonsful of genovese sauce, then fill the dish with the remaining tagliolini.
5. Generously spoon more genovese sauce over the surface and sprinkle with grated parmigiano, the remaining breadcrumbs, pepper and dots of butter.
6. Bake at 400°F / 200°C Gas Mark 6 for 30 minutes.
7. Remove from the oven and allow to rest for 15 minutes before serving.

SUGGESTED WINES:
Lacryma Christi del Vesuvio DOC (white) - Campania

TIMBALLO DI MACCHERONI

Savory shortbread, see recipe on page 73	1 lb/500 gr
Ragù, see recipe on page 84	2 qt/2 lt
Little meatballs, see recipe on page 83	10 ½ oz/300 gr
Butter	¼ cup/100 gr
Ziti	2 lb/1 kg
Fresh mozzarella or provola (smoked mozzarella)	10 ½ oz/300 gr
Salami	3 ½ oz/100 gr, diced
Hard boiled eggs	6, sliced
Breadcrumbs	as needed
Grated parmigiano	3 ½ cup/100 gr

1. Grease a tall ring pan with smooth sides. Dust all the inner surfaces with breadcrumbs.
2. Roll out the savory shortbread and line the inside of the ring pan with it.
3. Cook the ziti in abundant boiling salted water, drain and dress with the ragù.
4. Arrange a layer of ziti about 1-1 1/2"/3-4 cm deep in the ring pan. Distribute half of the mozzarella cut into small pieces, 1/3 of the meatballs, the salame and the hard boiled eggs. Spoon more ragù over the filling and sprinkle with grated parmigiano.
5. Cover the filling with another layer of ziti and distribute more mozzarella, another 1/3 of the meatballs, salami and hard boiled eggs over the pasta.
6. Fill to the top of the ring pan with the rest of the ziti and cover with a sheet of savory shortbread, cutting away the excess and sealing the edges, pinching them with your fingers.
7. Brush the top with an egg yolk beaten with a little water, then sprinkle generously with grated parmigiano.
8. Bake at 350°F/180°C/Gas Mark 4 for 45 minutes.
9. Remove from the oven and allow to cool for half an hour before turning it over onto a serving dish and removing the ring pan.
10. Fill the central hole with the remaining meatballs, decorate the serving dish with slices of hard boiled egg.
11. Serve with piping hot ragù and grated parmigiano.

SUGGESTED WINES:
Copertino DOC (red) - Puglia
Pollino Rosso Rubino DOC - Calabria

TRENETTE AL PESTO

Trenette or linguine	1 lb / 500 gr	Garlic	2 cloves
Fresh basil leaves	3 ½ oz / 100 gr, washed and dried	Grated parmigiano	½ oz / 100 gr
		Extra virgin olive oil	as needed
Pinoli (pine nuts)	3 ½ cup / 100 gr	Salt and pepper	to taste

1. Cook the trenette or linguine in abundant boiling salted water and drain when al dente.
2. Place all the ingredients in the food processor, retaining one half of the grated parmigiano and a few leaves of basil, and process until you have a smooth, homogenous sauce.
3. Dress the trenette and serve with a generous dusting of grated parmigiano and freshly ground black pepper.

SUGGESTED WINES:
Cinque Terre DOC (white) - Liguria

TUBETTI CON PISELLI
Tubetti with Green Peas

Tubetti (ditali or ditalini)	10 ½ oz / 300 gr
Fresh green peas	10 ½ oz / 300 gr, shelled
Spring onions	3 ½ oz / 100 gr, very thinly sliced
Extra virgin olive oil	½ cup / 100 cc
Butter	¼ cup / 50 gr
Pancetta	1 ¾ oz / 100 gr, finely diced
Dry white wine	½ cup / 100 cc
Salt and pepper	to taste

1. Melt the butter in the e.v.o.o. and sauté the onions.
2. When the onions become transparent, add the wine and reduce. Add the pancetta and sauté for 5 minutes.
3. Add the peas, salt and pepper and cover with hot water. Stir well.
4. Cook, covered, until the peas are about halfway done. Uncover and continue to cook until almost all the liquids have evaporated and the peas become creamy.
5. Add the tubetti which have been cooked in abundant salted boiling water until very al dente. Drain, letting them retain some of the water, and mix in with the peas.
6. Stir well, cover and allow to rest for 5 minutes before serving.

SUGGESTED WINES:
Frascati Superiore DOC (white) - Lazio

VERMICELLI AMMOLLICATI

Vermicelli are thick spaghetti. "Ammollicati" means made with stale bread without the crusts. A popular dish in the South, this is my own version.

Vermicelli or spaghetti	1 lb/500 gr
Sun dried tomatoes	7 oz/200 gr, reconstitued in e.v.o.o.
Green olives	½ cup/100 gr, pitted
Capers	1 tablespoon, washed in tepid water to remove the salt, dried.
Garlic	4 cloves
Hot chili pepper	a pinch
Stale bread deprived of its crust	7 oz/200 gr
Extra virgin olive oil	as needed
Salt	to taste
Dry white wine	¼ cup 50 cc
Grated parmigiano	to taste

1. While the pasta cooks, prepare the sauce:
2. Place all the ingredients but the bread in the food processor and chop coarsely. If you don't have a food processor you can do this by hand.
3. Heat a little e.v.o.o. in a pan and sauté all the chopped ingredients. When they've released their flavors to the oil, pour in the wine and reduce, stirring occasionally.
4. Warm a little e.v.o.o. in a small saucepan. When it's warm, crumble the bread into it and, shaking and stirring, brown the coarse breadcrumbs until nicely golden.
5. Drain the pasta when it's al dente and toss into the large pan. Mix well. Add the breadcrumbs and continue to toss and mix well. Serve hot with grated parmigiano.

SUGGESTED WINES:
Frascati Superiore DOC (white) - Lazio

ZITI AL TONNO
Ziti with Tuna

Ziti	1 lb/500 gr
Tuna in olive oil, drained	10 ½ oz/300 gr
Dry white wine	1 cup - 200 cc
Extra virgin olive oil	½ cup/100 cc
Onion	1 large, thinly sliced
Garlic	2 cloves, thinly sliced
Curry powder	a pinch
Fresh flat leaf parsley	2 tablespoons
Tomato paste	4 tablespoons
Salt and pepper	to taste

1. Sautè the onion and garlic with a pinch of curry in the e.v.o.o.
2. Add the tuna, breaking apart with a fork. Sauté, allowing the flavors to blend, then add the tomato paste which will have been dilluted in the wine, salt and pepper.
3. Reduce the sauce. Toss in the ziti which have been cooked in abundant salted boiling water and drained al dente.
4. Sauté for a minute or two over high heat, tossing and mixing to marry all the flavors.
5. Remove from the heat, mix in the chopped parsley and serve piping hot.

SUGGESTED WINES:
Frascati Superiore DOC (white) - Lazio

ZITONI ALL'INFERNO
The Devil's Ziti

FOR THE BÉCHAMEL:

Milk	1 qt/1 lt, hot	Flour	2 heaping
Butter	¼ cup/50 gr		tablespoons
Extra virgin olive oil	as needed	Onion	1 small, thinly sliced

1. In a small saucepan, lightly sauté the onion in a little e.v.o.o.
2. Add the butter.
3. When the butter has melted, add the flour stirring and mix well.
4. Slowly pour in the hot milk, stirring continuously, until the sauce has thickened.
5. Salt to taste.

Zitoni (large ziti)	1 lb/500 gr	Provola	10 ½ oz/300 gr,
Mixed fresh	1 lb/500 gr,	*(smoked mozzarella)*	
mushrooms	chopped coarsely	*refrigerated for a*	
Hot chili pepper	to taste	*couple of days, sliced*	
Spicy sausage	1 lb/500 gr	Extra virgin olive oil	as needed
Garlic	1 clove	Butter	as needed
Breadcrumbs	¼ cup/50 gr	Salt	to taste
Grated parmigiano	¼ cup/50 gr		

1. Cook the sausages with enough water to cover in a saucepan. When the water has dried, brown the sausages, then set aside. When they have cooled, slice the sausages.
2. Sautè the mushrooms, uncovered, in a little e.v.o.o. with garlic and the hot chili pepper over a high flame. The mushrooms will release their water. When the water evaporates and the mushrooms have browned, remove the garlic.
3. Mix the ziti, which have been cooked al dente in abundant boiling salted water, with the mushrooms and the béchamel.
4. Put half of the dressed ziti in a bakind dish. Spread a few spoonsful of the béchamel over the pasta.
5. Distribute the sliced sausages and the provola over the pasta.
6. Cover with the rest of the ziti. Dust the surface with breadcrumbs, grated parmigiano and dots of butter.
7. Bake at 350°F/180°C/Gas Mark 4 for 45 minutes.
8. When the surface has become golden brown and crisp, remove from the oven and let rest for 15 minutes before serving.

SUGGESTED WINES:
Pollino Rosso Rubino DOC - Calabria

Second Course:
Meat, poultry, fish, etc.

Unless otherwise indicated, the recipes are for 4-6 people

AGNELLO AL FORNO
Roast Lamb

Leg of lamb	2 ¼ lb / 1 kg, in pieces
Potatoes	2 ¼ lb / 1 kg, cut into wedges
Extra virgin olive oil	3 ¼ oz / 100 gr
Garlic	2 cloves, chopped
Dry white wine	¾ cup / 200 cc
Fresh flat leaf parsley	1 tablespoon, chopped
Onion	1, chopped
Rosemary	1 sprig fresh or 1 tablespoon dried
Lemons	2
Wine vinegar	2 tablespoons
Salt and pepper	to taste

1. Refrigerate the lamb overnight in a marinade of water, lemon, and vinegar.
2. Remove the lamb from the marinade and pat dry.
3. Place in a roasting pan with the potatoes, e.v.o.o., garlic, salt, pepper, parsley, onion, rosemary and wine.
4. Roast at 400°F/200°C/Gas Mark 6 for 40 minutes, turning over and basting frequently. When the meat and the potatoes are nicely browned, the liquids absorbed and the juices have formed a lovely gloss, remove from the oven and serve hot.

- At Easter, kid can be served interchangeably with lamb.

SUGGESTED WINES:
Leverano Rosso DOC - Puglia
Chianti Rufina DOCG - Toscana

ALICI GRATINATE
Fresh Anchovies Gratin

Fresh anchovies	2 ¼ lb / 1 kg, cleaned and scaled
Extra virgin olive oil	¼ cup / 50 cc
Fresh flat leaf parsley	2 tablespoons, chopped
Garlic	1 clove, thinly sliced
Breadcrumbs	½ cup / 100 gr
Salt	to taste
Organic lemon	1, cut into wedges

1. Grease a 10" / 25 cm baking dish with e.v.o.o.
2. Delicately arrange the anchovies in the dish.
3. Drizzle with e.v.o.o. then cover with the parsley and garlic.
4. Another generous drizzle of e.v.o.o. then sprinkle generously with the bread-crumbs, salt and pepper and a squeeze of lemon juice.
5. Bake at 440°F / 220°C / Gas Mark 7 for 10 minutes, until the surface is golden.
6. Serve hot with lemon wedges

SUGGESTED WINES:
Campi Flegrei Falanghina DOC - Campania

ALICI INDORATE E FRITTE
Breaded and Fried Fresh Anchovies

Large fresh anchovies	21 oz/600 gr
Extra virgin olive oil	3 ½ oz/100 gr
Flour	½ cup/100 gr
Eggs	4, beaten
Salt	to taste
Lemon	1

1. Delicately butterfly the anchovies. Clean, removing the heads.
2. Wash and dry the fish.
3. Dust very thoroughly in the flour, then dredge in the egg.
4. As the anchovies are breaded, place them delicately in a pan with the hot e.v.o.o. and fry them until they are golden, turning them once. Each anchovy will be cooked in one minute or less.
5. Lay them on paper towels to absorb any excess oil.
6. Serve hot, with lemon wedges.
7. Fried anchovies are well accompanied by a simple fresh salad.

SUGGESTED WINES:

Cinque Terre Bianco DOC - Liguria

ARISTA
Roast pork

Pork loin roast with bone	2 ¼ lb/1 kg
Pancetta	3 ½ oz/100 gr
Extra virgin olive oil	½ cup/100 gr
Dry white wine	½ cup/100 cc
Rosemary	2 sprigs fresh or 1 tablespoon dry
Sage	4 or 5 leaves fresh or 1 tablespoon dry
Garlic	4 cloves
Wild fennel seed	1 teaspoon
Salt and pepper	to taste

1. Chop together the rosemary, wild fennel seeds, garlic and sage.
2. Rub the roast with salt and pepper.
3. Cut away the bone but not completely. Holding the meat away from the bone, spread the herb blend all over the cavity.
4. Truss the roast using butcher's twine and place in a baking pan with the e.v.o.o. and the wine.
5. Roast at 350°F/180°C/Gas Mark 4 for 1 hour, basting regularly.

SUGGESTED WINES:
Montepulciano d'Abruzzo DOC - Abruzzo
Rosso di Montalcino DOC - Toscana

BACCALÀ ALLA PIZZAIOLA

Baccalà (salt-cured cod) of the best qualty	21 oz/600 gr, soaked in water and deprived of its salt
Tomato purée	2 cups/400 gr
Garlic	4 cloves, thinly sliced
Extra virgin olive oil	½ cup/100 gr
Salted capers	¼ cup/50 gr, washed in tepid water to deprive them of their salt
Gaeta olives	½ cup/100 gr, pitted and torn in half
Anchovy filets	4, chopped
Oregano	2 tablespoons
Pepper	to taste

1. Baccalà is sold dried or already soaked and de-salted. It's much easier to buy it this way than to buy it dry and soak it yourself. If you can't find it already soaked, choose the best quality baccalà available. It should be about 1"/2 ½ cm thick, its flesh should be white and its texture dry but pliable, not woody. Soak the baccalà at least 12 hours, changing the water 3 or 4 times. In summertime, keep it refrigerated during the soaking process. Wash, skin and de-bone the baccalà.
2. Cut the baccalà into pieces of equal size, about 1 ¾ oz/50 gr each.
3. Place the pieces of baccalà in a baking dish with a little e.v.o.o.
4. Sprinkle it with the olives, capers, anchovies.
5. Pour the tomato purèe over all, then sprinkle the surface with the sliced garlic and the oregano.
6. Drizzle e.v.o.o. over all.
7. Bake at 350°F/180°C/Gas Mark 4 for 40 minutes.
8. Serve hot or slightly warm.

- A variation of this dish is to dredge the pieces of baccalà in flour then dip in beaten egg yolks and quickly fry them before preparing the recipe as shown above. Don't fry the fish long enough to cook it, just enough that the breading is golden.

SUGGESTED WINES:
Castel San Lorenzo Rosato DOC - Campania
Taburno Greco DOC - Campania

BACCALÀ DI ZIA MARISA
Aunt Marisa's Baccalà

This dish is the recipe of Marisa Pallotta Alfani

Baccalà, thick and of the best quality	2 ¼ lb/1 kg, soaked in water and deprived of its salt
Potatoes	2 ¼ lb/1 kg, thickly sliced
Whole milk	1 qt/1 lt
All purpose flour	½ cup/100 gr
Fresh flat leaf parsley	3 tablespoons, chopped
Breadcrumbs	½ cup/100 gr
Extra virgin olive oil	¼ cup/50 gr
Pepper	to taste

1. Baccalà is sold dried or already soaked and de-salted. It's much easier to buy it this way than to buy it dry and soak it yourself. If you can't find it already soaked, choose the best quality baccalà available. It should be about 1"/2 ½ cm thick, its flesh should be white and its texture dry but pliable, not woody. Soak the baccalà at least 12 hours, changing the water 3 or 4 times. In summertime, keep it refrigerated during the soaking process.
2. Wash, skin and de-bone the baccalà, then cut it into 8 pieces of equal size.
3. Dust the fish with flour.
4. Place the potatoes in a baking dish that's been greased with e.v.o.o., cover them with the milk, then arrange the baccalà over the potatoes. Drizzle with e.v.o.o.
5. Sprinkle with freshly ground pepper, parsley and breadcrumbs.
6. Bake at 350°F/180°C/Gas Mark 4 on the bottom oven rack for 40 minutes or until the milk has been absorbed.

SUGGESTED WINES:
Lacryma Christi del Vesuvio bianco DOC - Campania
Gioia del Colle Bianco DOC - Puglia

BOCCONCINI DI VITELLO O POLLO
Veal or Chicken Morsels

Veal or boneless chicken	1 lb / 500 gr
All purpose flour	as needed
Extra virgin olive oil	¼ cup
Garlic	1 clove
Spring onions	4
Dry porcini mushrooms	¼ cup / 50 gr
Dry white wine	½ cup / 100 cc
Tomato paste	1 tablespoon
Salt and pepper	to taste

1. Soak the porcini mushrooms in tepid water for 20 minutes.
2. Drain the porcini, squeeze all the water from them and chop finely.
3. Cut the meat into 1 ¼" / 3 cm cubes.
4. Dust the meat with flour.
5. Sauté the onions and garlic in the e.v.o.o. When they become transparent, add the meat.
6. Sautè the meat, turning frequently, browning it evenly.
7. Add the mushrooms.
8. Cook together over medium heat for a few minutes, then add the tomato paste which will have been diluted in the wine and the chopped parsley.
9. Mix well, continue cooking over medium heat until the wine has reduced and the sauce has become smooth.

- To accompany this dish, I recommend a potato purée, roasted potatoes or fried artichokes.

SUGGESTED WINES:
Valtellina Rosso DOC - Lombardia
Lambrusco di Sorbara DOC - Emilia Romagna

CALAMARI FRITTI
Fried Calamari

Small fresh calamari,	1 lb / 500 gr, cleaned
no longer than	4″ / 10 cm
All purpose flour	1 cup / 200 gr
Extra virgin olive oil	2 ½ cups – 500 cc
Salt – to taste	
Lemon - 1	

1. Ask your fishmonger to clean the calamari for you.
2. Cut the calamari into rings 1/4″ / ½ cm wide, leaving the tentacles intact.
3. Wash well under running cold water, pat dry and refrigerate for at least one hour.
4. Dust in flour then quickly fry in very hot oil
5. As soon as they become golden, remove them with a slotted spoon or a skimmer and place on paper towels to absorb the oil.
6. Sprinkle with salt and serve hot, with lemon wedges.

- As a side, I like to serve a very simple fresh green salad dressed with e.v.o.o. and lemon.

SUGGESTED WINES:
Lacryma Christi del Vesuvio bianco - Campania
Gioia del Colle Bianco - Puglia

CAPPONE AL BURRO ALLA LATOUR
Latour Family's Capon in Butter Sauce

From the recipe of my Belgian great-grandmother,
Emilie Latour Alfani (second half of the 19th century)

Capon	4 ½ lb / 2 kg
Butter	¾ cup / 200 gr
Green olives	2 cups / 300 gr
Dry white wine	1 cup / 250 cc
All purpose flour	3 heaping tablespoons
Bay leaves	6
Salt and pepper	to taste
Hot water	enough to cover the capon

1. Put the capon cut into pieces, along with all the ingredients, except for the flour and the salt, in a dutch oven and cook, covered, for 2 hours over low heat.
2. Thin the flour with a little of the broth that has formed in the pot, and add it with the salt, mixing it in delicately. Uncover and cook for another hour over a low flame, stirring occasionally.
3. After three hours, the sauce should be dense and creamy, and the capon so tender it falls from the bone.

- The best pot to cook this in is one made of terra cotta.
- This is a tasty and satisfying dish for a winter pranzo. I like to serve it with tender peas, ramequins or a potato purée.

SUGGESTED WINES:

Sannio Greco Bianco DOC - Campania
Muller Thurgau DOC - Trentino Alto Adige

CARNE ALLA GLACE DI NONNA LINA
Nonna Lina's Round of Beef alla Glace

From Orsola Farina Alfani, my grandmother

Round of beef	4 ½ lb / 2 kg, trussed with butcher's twine
Butter	7 oz / 200 gr
Extra virgin olive oil	1 ¾ oz / 50 gr
All purpose flour	1 ¾ oz / 50 gr
Dry white wine	¾ cup / 200 cc
Tomato paste	2 tablespoons
Carrots	2, finely chopped
Onions	2, finely chopped
Celery	1 stalk, finely chopped
Garlic	1 clove, finely chopped
Salt	to taste

1. Melt the butter in the e.v.o.o., then lightly sautè the carrots, onions, celery and garlic. When the onion becomes transparent, lay the meat over the vegetables and brown it on all sides.
2. Add the tomato paste dissolved in the wine and two glasses of hot water.
3. Cover and cook on low heat for one hour.
4. Remove the meat to a platter and allow it to cool - it's easier to slice when the meat has cooled a bit.
5. Add the flour, salt and a lump of butter the size of a walnut to the pot, stir briskly and continuously as the liquids reduce and the sauce becomes velvety.
6. Pass the sauce through a food mill.
7. Slice the meat as thickly or thinly as you prefer, then return them to the pot with the sauce and cook for 10 minutes.

- The best accompaniments for this dish are a potato purée and tender peas cooked with spring onion.
- This is a delicate *secondo*, the perfect choice for an elegant lunch or dinner.

SUGGESTED WINES:
Garda Pinot Noir DOC - Veneto
Barbera d'Alba DOC - Piemonte

CINGHIALE ALLA CACCIATORA
Wild boar, hunter style

After the hunt, the men would cook up a meal with the game they'd just bagged or, better still, take it home for their women to prepare it, simmering the game with their gardens' vegetables and the wild mushrooms that they would find in their surrounding woods

Wild boar shoulder	1 lb / 1 kg, cut into 1 ¼" / 3 cm cubes
Dried porcini mushrooms	⅓ cup / 60 gr,
(soaked in warm water, drained and squeezed of all excess liquid then chopped coarsely)	
Fresh mixed mushrooms	1lb / 500 gr, coarsely chopped or sliced
Fresh tomatoes	1lb / 500 gr, peeled, seeded and coarsely chopped
Yellow onions	2, sliced
Garlic	2 cloves, chopped
Rosemary, sage and bay leaves tied into a bouquet	
Dry red wine	½ cup / 100 cc
Red wine vinegar	1 tablespoon
All purpose flour	½ cup / 100 gr
Extra virgin olive oil	½ cup / 100 cc
Salt and pepper	to taste

1. Prepare a marinade with e.v.o.o., wine, vinegar, onion, garlic, pepper and herbs.
2. Toss the meat in the marinade. After 2-3 hours, drain the meat, pat it dry with paper towels, dredge in the flour and brown in e.v.o.o.
3. Add the dried porcini. After a few minutes, add the fresh mushrooms.
4. Cook the mushrooms together for several minutes, then add the tomatoes.
5. After 15 minutes, add the marinade with all its herbs. Continue cooking, stirring frequently, until the sauce reduces to a creamy consistency.
6. Remove the herb bouquet. Use a slotted spoon to plate the wild boar and mushrroms. Strain the sauce and spoon over the meat.
7. Accompany with roasted potatoes and green beans sautéed with garlic.

SUGGESTED WINES:
Brunello di Montalcino DOCG - Toscana
Montefalco Sagrantino DOCG - Umbria

CINGHIALE UBRIACO
Drunken Wild Boar

Boneless leg of wild boar	2 ¼ lb/1 kg
All purpose flour	1 cup/200 gr
Red or black grapes	1 bunch
Onion	1, chopped
Chestnuts	10 ½ oz/300 gr, husked, boiled and peeled
Walnuts	10, shelled
Aged balsamic vinegar	2 tablespoons
Extra virgin olive oil	¼ cup/50 gr
Tomato paste	½ cup/100 gr
Red wine	½ cup/100 cc
Rosemary	1 sprig fresh or 1 tablespoon dried
Garlic	3 cloves, chopped
Salt and pepper	to taste

1. Cut the meat into uniform cubes about the size of an egg and dust them in the flour.
2. Cook together with the onion and garlic on low heat for 30 minutes until nicely browned.
3. Add the tomato paste that's been dissolved in the wine, the balsamic, the grapes, chestnuts, walnuts, salt, pepper and rosemary. Retain some of the grapes, chestnuts and walnuts for the garnish.
4. Cook, covered, over low heat for one hour.
5. Uncover and keep cooking until the liquids reduce and the sauce thickens slightly.
6. Serve decorated with a sauce prepared with raw grapes, the walnut halves and boiled chestnuts cooked for 5 minutes in a little bit of the boar's gravy.

- When grapes chestnuts are out of season, substitute with a sauce made of a full bodied red wine (1 ¼ cup/250cc reduced to half) and use dried chestnuts soaked in water for several hours.
- Ideal accompaniments are roasted potatoes and boiled green beans.

SUGGESTED WINES:
Aglianico del Vulture Rosso DOC - Basilicata
Controguerra Rosso DOC - Abruzzo

COTOLETTE AL FORNO
CON MOZZARELLA E PROSCIUTTO
Baked Veal Cutlets with Mozzarella & Prosciutto

Veal cutlets	1 ¼ lb / 600 gr
Flour	½ cup / 100 gr
Breadcrumbs	½ cup / 100 gr
Eggs	2, lightly beaten and salted
Extra virgin olive oil	2 tablespoons / 25 cc
Butter	¼ cup / 50 gr
Mozzarella	7 oz / 200 gr, sliced
Prosciutto	7 oz / 200 gr, thinly sliced
Fresh sage leaves	as needed, chopped
Salt and pepper	to taste

1. Dredge the cutlets in flour then dip them in the beaten eggs.
2. Dust well with the breadcrumbs, patting them firmly with your hands to be sure the breadcrumbs stick.
3. Arrange the cutlets in a baking dish in which the butter has been melted with the e.v.o.o.
4. Arrange the prosciutto on the cutlets, then cover with the mozzarella.
5. Cover with the chopped sage.
6. Bake at 400°F 200°C / Gas Mark 6 for 15 minutes, basting each cutlet when they are halfway cooked.
7. Serve hot.

SUGGESTED WINES:
Taburno Piedirosso DOC - Campania
Parrina Rosso DOC - Toscana

COTOLETTE ALLA FRANCESE
Veal or Chicken Cutlets alla Francese

Veal or chicken cutlets	1 ¼ lb / 600 gr, 1/4″ / ½ cm thick
Flour	½ cup / 100 gr
Grated parmigiano	1 cup / 200 gr
Salt and pepper	to taste
Eggs	2, lightly beaten and salted
Extra virgin olive oil	2 tablespoons / 25 cc
omato purée	2 cups / 500 gr
Fresh basil	2 tablespoons, chopped
	retain a few leaves for garnish

FOR THE LIGHT TOMATO SAUCE:
1. Cook the purée in a saucepan with a little salt, the basil and a tablespoon of e.v.o.o.
2. Allow it to reduce for about 10 minutes, stirring frequently.
3. Keep the sauce hot.

FOR THE CUTLETS:
1. Dredge the cutlets in flour, patting with your hands to adhere the flour to the meat.
2. Dip in the beaten egg then delicately dredge in the grated parmigiano.
3. Return the cutlets to the egg and dredge once more in the parmigiano.
4. Fry the cutlets over a high flame, turning them once.
5. When they are cooked, place them on paper towels to drain the excess oil.
6. Arrange a spoon or two of the tomato sauce on each dish and place the cutlets over the sauce. Decorate with a little more sauce and some basil leaves. Sprkinkle with parmigiano.

SUGGESTED WINES:
Chianti Colli Senesi DOCG - Toscana
Galatina Rosso DOC - Puglia

FILETTO DI MAIALE
AL PEPE VERDE E COGNAC
Pork Tenderloin with Green Peppercorns & Cognac

A very tasty and sophisticated dish

Pork tenderloin	1 ¾ lb / 800 gr, cut into 8 medallions
Flour	½ cup / 100 gr
Extra virgin olive oil	¼ cup / 50 cc
Butter	¼ cup / 50 gr
Scallion or green onion	1 medium, chopped
Fresh sage	as you like
Green peppercorns	2 tablespoons
Cognac	to taste

1. Dredge the pork medallions in flour, shaking off the excess flour, and cook in the butter and e.v.o.o. for 5 minutes on one side, 3 minutes on the other.
2. Remove from the pan to a warm platter.
3. Add the onion to the pan and sauté.
4. When the onion is transparent, add salt to taste, the peppercorns and the sage.
5. Allow the sauce to cook for 5 minutes over medium heat, then return the meat to the pan.
6. Cook for 10 minutes, turning the meat over once.
7. When the meat is cooked, uncover, add the cognac and allow it to reduce, mixing well.

- The ideal side for this dish is pommes dauphine, see recipe on page 279

SUGGESTED WINES:
Sangiovese di Romagna DOC - Emilia Romagna
Albugnano Superiore DOC - Piemonte

ORATA UBRIACA
Drunken Sea Bream

Fresh sea bream or sea bass	3-4 lb / 1 ½-2 kg, scaled and cleaned
Unripe green grapes	1 bunch
Grape leaves	6-8
Bay leaves	2-3
Lemon	1, sliced thinly
Extra virgin olive oil	as needed
Dry white wine	¼ cup – 50 cc
Salt	to taste
Pink peppercorns	20
Parchment paper to wrap the fish in for baking	

1. Rinse the fish in cold water, pat dry.
2. Lightly season the fish, inside the cavity as well as outside, with e.v.o.o. and salt.
3. Carefully insert the bunch of grapes, the peppercorns, bay leaves and 3 slices of lemon inside the cavity.
4. Spread a sheet of parchment paper over the baking pan.
5. Place half of the grape leaves and and the lemon slices on the parchment paper, then place the fish over the lemon slices.
6. Pour the wine over the fish then cover the fish with the other half of the grape leaves.
7. Fold the parchment paper like an envelope, enclosing the fish such that the juices will be sealed inside.
8. Bake at 350°F/180°C/Gas Mark 4 for 30 minutes.
9. Remove from the oven and allow to stand for about 10 minutes.
10. Carefully take the fish in its parchment envelope, place it on a serving dish and take it to the table where your guests will enjoy the fragrances that are released when you open the parchment envelope!
11. Serve each portion accompanied with the peppercorns and grapes and a spoon of the fish's juices.

- The drunken sea bream is nicely accompanied by boiled potatoes and brussels sprouts.

SUGGESTED WINES:
Bolgheri Rosato DOC - Toscana
Lacryma Christi del Vesuvio DOC - Campania

MAIALE CON PATATE E PEPERONI
Pork Ribs with Potatoes & Peppers

Pork spare ribs	1 ¼ lb / 600 gr
Potatoes	1 lb / 500 gr, sliced into discs
Pickled peppers	10 ½ oz / 300 gr, deprived of their seeds and cut into medium sized pieces
Dry white wine	¼ cup / 50 cc
Extra virgin olive oil	½ cup / 100 cc
Salt	to taste

1. Fry the potatoes and remove them to a dish lined with paper towels to absorb the excess oil.
2. Remove the seeds from the peppers. Cut them into pieces.
3. Fry the ribs. A few minutes before they are cooked, pour in the wine.
4. When the wine has reduced, add the peppers and return the potatoes to the pan.
5. Add salt to taste and cook, tossing and stirring for 4-5 minutes.
6. Serve hot.

SUGGESTED WINES:
Solopaca Rosso DOC - Campania
Chianti Classico Riserva Casamonti DOCG - Toscana

PEPOSO

An ancient dish from the village of Impruneta, near Florence

Lean beef	1 ¾ lb / 800 gr, cubed
Flour	½ cup / 100 gr
Extra virgin olive oil	½ cup / 100 gr
Tomato paste	½ cup / 100 gr
Garlic	4 cloves
Rosemary and bay leaves	to taste
Chianti Classico wine	1 ½ cups / 500 cc
Salt	to taste
Black peppercorns	2 tablespoons, cracked

1. Dredge the cubed beef in the flour.
2. Brown the garlic and the meat in the e.v.o.o.
3. Add the tomato paste which will have been dissloved in the wine, salt and the cracked peppercorns.
4. Add enough hot water to cover and cook, covered, over medium-low heat for one hour, stirring occasionally.
5. Uncover, cook for another 30 minutes.
6. If the sauce isn't dense enough, remove the meat and reduce it until it thickens.
7. Serve with mashed or roasted potatoes and green beans sautéed with garlic.

SUGGESTED WINES:
Chianti Classico Riserva Fattoria Montagliari DOCG - Toscana

POLLO ALL'ARANCIA DI EMILIE
Chicken in Orange Sauce

from the recipe of Emilie Latour Alfani

Chicken thighs	1 ¼ lb / 600 gr, deboned
Flour	½ cup / 100 gr
Extra virgin olive oil	¼ cup / 50 cc
Butter	¼ cup / 50 gr
Organic oranges	2
Honey of your choice	2 tablespoons
Grand Marnier or Cointreau	to taste
Salt and pepper	to taste
Pink peppercorns	to taste

1. Dredge the chicken in flour, patting it with the palms of your hands to make the flour stick to it.
2. Melt the butter with the e.v.o.o. in a large pan.
3. Add the chicken and cook over medium heat for 5 minutes.
4. Turn the chicken over and cook another 3 minutes.
5. Remove the chicken to a warm platter.
6. Add the honey, salt, pepper and, cognac or Cointreau and the juice of one of the oranges to the pan.
7. Reduce the sauce over medium heat, stirring, for a few minutes, then return the chicken to the pan.
8. Toss the chicken well to coat it with the sauce, then cover, reduce the heat and cook for 10 minutes.
9. Uncover, stir the chicken and cook for two more minutes, allowing the sauce to thicken.
10. Slice the other orange and arrange them on the plates. Serve the chicken with its sauce over the orange slices.

SUGGESTED WINES:
Terre di Franciacorta Rosso DOC - Lombardia
Contessa Entellina Ansonica Bianco DOC - Sicilia

POLLO ALLA CACCIATORA
Chicken alla Cacciatora

Instead of chicken, this dish can be prepared using rabbit–and in place of the mushrooms, red or yellow bell peppers

Chicken thighs, or any meat you prefer	2 ¼ lb / 1kg
Dried porcini	2 oz / 60gr, soaked, drained, squeezed dry and chopped
Fresh porcini or mixed mushrooms	12 oz / 300gr
Peeled tomotoes	20 oz / 500gr, cleaned of their seeds and chopped
Yellow onions, sliced	2
Red bell peppers	2 or 3
Garlic	2 cloves, chopped
Rosemary, sage and bay leaves tied into a bouquet	
Dry red wine	
Red wine vinegar	1 tablespoon
Flour	½ cup / 100gr
Extra virgin olive oil	½ cup / 100 cc
Salt and pepper	as needed

1. Prepare a marinade with the e.v.o.o., the wine, vinegar, onions, garlic, pepper and the bouquet of herbs.
2. Debone the meat and cut into cubes about 1 1/4" 3cm. Marinate it for 1 hour.
3. Drain the meat and blot it dry with paper towels.
4. Dredge the meat in flour and brown in the e.v.o.o. over a medium-high flame.
5. Add the dried porcini mushrooms.
6. Sauté for a few minutes, then add fresh mushrooms and/or peppers cut roughly into medium sized pieces.
7. Cook, allowing the flavors to blend, then add the tomatoes.
8. Add the marinade and cook, uncovered, for 15 minutes over medium heat, stirring often, until the sauce reduces and becomes velvety.
9. Remove the herb bouquet and serve the stew with the sauce and vegetables spooned over it.
10. The "cacciatora" is well accompanied by roast potatoes and white beans dressed in garlicy olive oil!

SUGGESTED WINES:
Chianti Classico Riserva DOCG - Toscana
Montefalco Sagrantino DOCG - Umbria

POLLO E PEPERONI IN AGRODOLCE
Sweet and Sour Chicken and Peppers

Chicken breasts and or thighs	1 ¼ lb/600 gr, deboned
Red bell peppers	1 ¼ lb/600 gr, sliced into strips
Lemons	2, juiced
Sugar	1 tablespoon
Extra virgin olive oil	¼ cup/50 cc
Flour	½ cup/100 gr
Tomato paste	1 tablespoon
White wine vinegar	2 tablespoons
Salt	to taste
Green peppercorns	1 tablespoon
Cognac	to taste

1. Marinate the chicken for one hour in the lemon juice dilluted in a bit of water.
2. Pat the chicken dry then lightly dredge the chicken in flour with a pinch of salt.
3. Warm the e.v.o.o. in a pan and add the chicken to brown on all sides. When it is nicely golden, remove to a warm platter.
4. Add the peppers and fry along with the chicken. When they are done, drain off the excess e.v.o.o. and add the vinegar, sugar and tomato paste.
5. Stir and toss rapidly to coat the peppers with the sauce.
6. Adjust salt if necessary.
7. Return the chicken to the pan.
8. Add the wine, the peppercorns and the cognac or brandy.
9. Allow the brandy to reduce, then cover, remove from the heat and let stand for five minutes.
10. Serve the chicken with the peppers on the side and the sauce with peppercorns.

- An ideal accompaniment is purèe of potatoes or potatoes dauphine (recipe on page 279)

SUGGESTED WINES:
Terre di Franciacorta Rosso DOC - Lombardia
Contessa Entellina Bianco DOC - Sicilia

POLPETTE AL POMODORO
Meatballs in Tomato Sauce

Lean ground beef	¾ lb/400 gr
Lean ground pork	¾ lb/400 gr
Ground prosciutto	3 ½ oz/100 gr
Day old bread with crusts removed	7 oz/200 gr, soaked in water then squeezed dry
Eggs	2
Grated parmigiano	½ cup/100 gr
Salt and pepper	to taste
Nutmeg	a pinch
Flour	½ cup/100 gr
Extra virgin olive oil	¾ cup/150 gr
Tomato purée	2 cups/500 gr
Fresh basil leaves	2 tablespoons, chopped

1. Prepare the simple tomato sauce: combine in a saucepan the tomato purée, a little e.v.o.o., a pinch of salt and the basil and cook for 10 minutes.
2. In a large mixing bowl, combine the meats with the bread, parmigiano, eggs, nutmeg, salt and pepper.
3. Mix well, refrigerate for one hour.
4. Using the palms of your hands, roll the meatballs to about the size of an egg.
5. Dredge the meatballs in flour then fry them in e.v.o.o., turning them so that they brown evenly.
6. Use a slotted spoon to remove them to a dish covered with paper towel.
7. When the excess oil has been absorbed by the paper towel, add them to the saucepan containing the tomato sauce. Try to arrange them so that they're in a single layer. Cook for 5 minutes.
8. Stir them delicately, lower the heat and cook for 5 more minutes.
9. Serve with fried potato wedges or fried breaded artichoke hearts.

SUGGESTED WINES:

Barbera d'Asti Rosso DOCG - Piemonte
Galluccio Rosso Riserva DOC - Campania

POLPETTE DI CARNE E PATATE
Meat and Potato Balls

Lean ground beef	10 ½ oz / 300 gr
Potatoes	10 ½ oz / 300 gr, boiled, peeled and mashed
Eggs	2
Grated parmigiano	½ cup / 100 gr
Fresh flat leaf parsley	2 tablespoons, chopped
Salt and pepper	to taste
Extra virgin olive oil	¼ cup / 50 cc
Butter	¼ cup / 50 cc

1. Mix together the meat, potatoes, parmigiano, salt, pepper and parsley.
2. Refrigerate for one hour.
3. Using the palms of your hands, roll each meatball into a ball the size of an egg.
4. Melt the butter in the e.v.o.o., then fry the meatballs until they are nicely browned on all sides and cooked in the middle.
5. Drain the cooked meatballs on paper towels to remove any excess oil.
6. They can be eaten hot or cold and are well accompanied by a fresh green salad.

SUGGESTED WINES:
Lacryma Christi del Vesuvio Rosso DOC - Campania
Vignanello Rosso Novello DOC - Lazio

POLPETTE DI POLLO
Chicken Meatballs

Skinned chicken thighs	6
Butter	½ cup / 100 gr
Pitted green olives	1 cup / 200 gr
Dry white wine	½ cup / 100 cc
Bay leaves	5
Eggs	2
Salte and pepper	to taste
Bread with the crust removed	10 ½ oz / 300 gr
Milk	as needed
Extra virgin olive oil	½ cup / 100 cc
Flour	½ cup / 100 gr

1. Dust the chicken and place them in a pan. Cover with cold water.
2. Add the butter, olives, bay leaves, wine, salt and pepper.
3. Cook for one hour, turning over the chicken frequently to keep it from sticking to the bottom of the pan.
4. When the chicken is cooked, the water will have reduced.
5. Debone the chicken and grind it in the food processor. Hold aside the sauce.
6. Allow to cool, then add the eggs, and the bread that's been soaked in milk then squeezed dry. Mix well.
7. Refrigerate for two hours or overnight.
8. Form little meatballs about the size of a walnut or larger, as you like. Dust them in flour and fry them in the e.v.o.o.
9. Serve with the sauce that you reserved from cooking the chicken.

- These chicken meatballs go very nicely with baby peas, or sautéed artichokes or mushrooms.
- You can prepare a meat loaf with this same recipe. Stuff it with hard boiled eggs, fontina cheese and prosciutto, then dust with flour and fry in e.v.o.o.

SUGGESTED WINES:
Capri Bianco DOC - Campania
Lacryma Christi del Vesuvio Bianco DOC - Campania

POLPETTONCINI CON SORPRESA
Little Meatloaves with a Surprise

Vegetable broth	1 qt / 1 lt, see recipe on page 67
Lean ground beef	1 ¼ lb / 600 gr
Day old bread	¾ lb / 300 gr, soaked in water then squeezed dry
Eggs	2
Hard boiled eggs	4
Egg white	1, lightly beaten
Salt and pepper	to taste
Fresh flat leaf parsley	2 tablespoons, chopped
Grated parmigiano	½ cup / 100 gr
Prosciutto	3 ½ oz / 100 gr
Flour	½ cup / 100 gr
Extra virgin olive oil	1 cup / 200 cc

1. Mix together the meat, bread, two eggs, parmigiano, salt and pepper.
2. Divide the mixture into four equal parts and form each one into a small loaf.
3. Wrap each hard boiled egg with prosciutto.
4. Use the side of your hand to form an indentation in each loaf and place a prosciutto-wrapped egg inside it. Then form the meat around the egg, returning it to its original loaf shape.
5. When all the four loaves have been stuffed with their "surprise", dredge them in flour, dip them in the lightly beaten egg white and fry them in hot oil, one or two at a time. Cook for 10 minutes, turning the loaves frequently so that they will brown evenly on all sides.
6. Remove the browned loaves to a baking dish just large enough to hold them comfortably. Pour in enough hot vegetable broth to cover them about half way and bake in an oven preheated to 400°F / 200°C / Gas Mark 6 for 30 minutes.
7. Remove the loaves to a platter, pour the juices into a saucepan. Add the wine, salt, pepper and chopped parsley and cook to reduce over a medium-high flame.
8. Serve one little loaf to each guest, with the sauce spooned over it.

- I like to accompany my surprise meat loaves with baby peas cooked with spring onion or green beans sautéed with garlic and parsley.

SUGGESTED WINES:
Barbera d'Asti Rosso DOCG - Piemonte
Montefalco Rosso DOC - Umbria

POLPETTONE DI TONNO E PATATE
Tuna and Potato Loaf

Tuna packed in olive oil	¾ lb/400 gr, drained
Potatoes	1 lb/500 gr, boiled and mashed
Eggs	2
Grated parmigiano	½ cup/100 gr
Bread crumbs	¼ cup/50 cc
Salt and pepper	to taste
Mayonaisse	as you like

1. Put the tuna through a meat grinder or chop it in a food processor.
2. In a mixing bowl, combine the tuna with the potatoes, eggs, parmigiano, bread crumbs, salt and pepper.
3. Mix well.
4. Cover the bowl with clear plastic wrap and refrigerate for a few hours. Remove the mixture from the refrigerator and shape it into a loaf.
5. Snuggly wrap the loaf in a clean cotton cloth that has been soaked and wrung dry and tie both ends of tightly with butcher's twine.
6. Fill a pot with enough water to barely cover the loaf. Bring the water to the boil.
7. When the water boils, gingerly place the loaf in the water. Lower the heat to a lively simmer and cook for 40 minutes.
8. Remove the loaf from the boiling water and allow to cool, then refrigerate it for at least two hours.
9. Remove the cloth and cut the loaf into slices 1/2"/1 cm thick.
10. Serve with mayonaisse

SUGGESTED WINES:
Etna Bianco DOC - Sicilia
Vernaccia di San Gimignano DOCG - Toscana

ROLLÈ DI VITELLA
Veal Rollé

Veal flank	2 ¼ lb/1 kg
Potatoes	2 ¼ lb/1 kg, cut into wedges
Garlic	1 clove, chopped
Fresh flat leaf parsley	1 tablespoon, chopped
Sage and rosemary	as you like
Onion	1, chopped
Dry white wine	½ cup/100 cc
Pancetta	3 ½ oz/100 gr, diced
Eggs	6, hard boiled
Semi-sweet Provolone cheese	7 oz/200 gr, in thin slices
Boiled ham	7 oz/200 gr
Salt and pepper	to taste
Extra virgin olive oil	as needed

1. Lay the meat out on your work surface.
2. Sprinkle it with salt and pepper to taste.
3. Arrange the sliced provolone and ham over the meat, then place the hard boiled eggs in a line down the center.
4. Roll the meat up, enclosing the stuffing in its center. Truss it firmly with butcher's twine.
5. Brown the veal roll in the e.v.o.o. along with the chopped garlic, onion and pancetta.
6. When it's been evenly browned, move everything to a roasting pan and add the potatoes, the wine, rosemary, sage, salt and pepper.
7. Roast in an oven that's been preheated to 400°F/200°C for 30 minutes, turning and basting 2 or 3 times.

SUGGESTED WINES:
Molise Rosso DOC - Molise
Morellino di Scansano DOCG - Toscana

SOGLIOLA ALLA MUGNAIA
Sole alla Mugnaia

Fresh sole	2, 10 ½ oz/300 gr each, scaled and cleaned
Butter	½ cup/100 gr
Extra virgin olive oil	3-4 tablespoons
Dry white wine	½ cup/100 cc
Organic lemons	2
Flour	½ cup/100 gr
Salt and pepper	to taste
Bread crumbs	2 tablespoons

1. Wash the fish well, remove the skin from the upper side and the scales from the bottom. Pat the fish dry.
2. Dredge in flour, patting firmly with the hands to adhere the flour.
3. Melt the butter in a pan and add the zest of one of the lemons along with its juice.
4. Place the fish in the pan with it's back facing up, and sprinkle with the bread-crumbs.
5. Add the wine and bake for 20 minutes at 400°F/200°C/Gas Mark 4.
6. Using a spatula, remove the fish to a warmed platter.
7. Reduce the cooking juices to a smooth sauce.
8. Serve the fish, fileted, with the sauce spooned over it and garnished with lemon slices.

SUGGESTED WINES:
Verdicchio di Matelica Bianco DOC - Marche
Circeo Bianco DOC - Lazio

SCALOPPINE AL MARSALA
Veal Scaloppine al Marsala

The recipe comes from Sicily, as does the delicious wine that gives it its distinctive flavor. In Tuscany this dish can be made with Vinsanto instead of Marsala, but no one can keep us from using Port of Sauterne if we like!

Veal cutlets	8, all the same size, 1 ¾ lb / 800 gr
Butter	½ cup / 100 gr
Extra virgin olive oil	¼ cup / 50 cc
Flour	½ cup / 100 gr
Dry Marsala wine	½ cup / 100 cc
Salt and pepper	to taste

1. Dust the cutlets in the flour then press with the palms of your hands to adhere the flour on while eliminating any extra.
2. Delicately place them in a pan in which you've already melted the butter in the e.v.o.o.
3. Cook over medium heat for two minutes, then turn over and cook another minute.
4. Remove the cutlets to a warm platter. Don't cover them!
5. Reduce the heat, add salt and pepper to the sauce that's formed in the pan
6. Add the marsala and reduce until the sauce has become velvety.
7. Raise the heat, return the cutlets to the pan and cook for 2-3 minutes, turning over once.
8. Serve hot accompanied by a potato purée.

- You can prepare this same recipe using beautiful swordfish steaks rather than veal.

SUGGESTED WINES:
Contessa Entellina Ansonica DOC (bianco) - Sicilia
Etna Bianco DOC (bianco) - Sicilia

SPEZZATINO DI BACCALÀ AL FORNO
Baked Baccala

Baccalà, thick and of the best qualty	2 ¼ lb / 1 kg, soaked in water
Potatoes	2 ¼ lb / 1 kg, thickly sliced
Capers	¼ cup / 50 gr
Oregano	1 tablespoon
Breadcrumbs	½ cup / 100 gr
Greek olives	7 oz / 200 gr, pitted
Extra virgin olive oil	¼ cup / 50 gr
Garlic	1 clove, finely chopped
Tomato paste	1 tablespoon

1. Baccalà is sold dried or already soaked and de-salted. It's much easier to buy it this way than to buy it dry and soak it yourself. If you can't find it already soaked, choose the best quality baccalà available. It should be about 1"/2 ½ cm thick, its flesh should be white and its texture dry but pliable, not woody. Soak the baccalà at least 12 hours, changing the water 3 or 4 times. In summertime, keep it refrigerated during the soaking process.
2. Wash, skin and de-bone the baccalà.
3. Cut the baccalà into medium size cubes.
4. In a baking dish, arrange the potatoes in a single layer, then the baccalà, the olives, capers, garlic, oregano, the tomato paste dissolved in the white wine.
5. Drizzle all with the e.v.o.o.
6. Sprinkle generously with breadcrumbs and bake at 400°F/200°C/Gas Mark 6 for 30 minutes or more, until the top has formed a lovely golden crust.

SUGGESTED WINES:
Frascati Bianco DOC - Lazio
Erbaluce di Calusco - Piemonte

SPEZZATINO DI VITELLA
Veal Stew

Lean tender veal	1 ¼ lb/600 gr, cubed
Extra virgin olive oil	¼ cup/50 cc
Tomato paste	4 tablespoons
Dry white wine	¼ cup/100 cc
Flour	3 ½ oz/100 gr
Shallots or spring onions	4-5, thinly sliced
Garlic	1 clove, chopped
Carrot	1, finely diced
Celery	1 stalk, finely diced
Salt and pepper	to taste

1. Dredge the cubed meat and brown in the e.v.o.o. along with the onion and garlic, stirring and tossing frequently.
2. Add the carrot and celery, and the tomato paste which has been dissolved in the wine.
3. Cook, uncovered, over low flame for 30 minutes, stirring frequently.
4. Add salt and pepper.
5. Reduce the juices to a creamy sauce and serve the stew with its sauce spooned over it.

SUGGESTED WINES:
Chianti Colli Senesi DOCG - Toscana, Montefalco Sagrantino DOCG - Umbria

TAGLIATA IN INFUSIONE
Sliced Steak Infusion

1. Grill the steak, preferrably on a wood burning barbecue.
2. When it is well charred on the outside and still very pink on the inside, salt and cut it into slices about 1/4" / 3/4cm thick.
3. Immediately submerge the sliced meat into a transparant cup or glass filled with e.v.o.o., a sprig of rosemary and several leaves of sage and laurel.
4. The cool oil will stop the meat from continuing to cook. The meat, having sat in this infusion, will be tender and delicious.

- The ideal accompaniment to this refined dish - potatoes roasted with e.v.o.o., rosemary and sage.

SUGGESTED WINES:
Chianti Classico Riserva Fattoria Montagliari DOCG - Toscana
Cerasuola di Vittoria DOCG - Sicilia

STRACOTTO DI MANZO
Stewed Beef

This stew, in Italian, is called "stracotto" which means over-cooked,
referring to the long, slow stewing process.

Lean beef shoulder	2 lb/1 kg, cubed
Pancetta	3 ½ oz/100 gr, diced
Salt	to taste
Oregano	a pinch
Tomato paste	4 ½ oz/125 gr
Tomato pulp	2 ½ cups/500 gr
Extra virgin olive oil	½ cup/100 cc

FOR THE MARINADE:

Dry red wine	¾ cup/125 cc
Onion	1, chopped
Celery	2 stalks, chopped
Carrots	2, chopped
Leek	1, chopped
Garlic	2 cloves
Dried porcini mushrooms	1 ¾ oz/ 50 gr, soaked and squeezed dry
Bay leaf	2 leaves
Fresh flat leaf parsley	a small bunch
Clove	1
Nutmeg	a pinch

1. Marinate the meat and the pancetta with all the chopped vegetables and the wine for 3 hours.
2. Drain from the marinade, pat dry and brown in hot e.v.o.o.
3. When the meat is nicely and evenly browned, add the marinade, the tomato pulp and paste. Mix well and cook over low heat for two hours, stirring frequently.
4. Remove the meat to a warmed platter and pass the sauce through a food mill.
5. Reduce the sauce over medium-high heat until it becomes a velvety sauce. Adjust the salt.
6. Serve the meat with sauce on the side. The extra sauce can be used to dress the pasta of your choice!

SUGGESTED WINES:
Vino Nobile di Montepulciano DOCG - Toscana
Valcalepio Rosso Riserva DOC - Lombardia

TRIGLIE ALLA VESUVIO
Red Snapper Vesuvio

Red snapper or similar fish	2 small
Tomato pulp	2 cups / 400 gr
Garlic	2 cloves, chopped
Extra virgin olive oil	½ cup / 100 cc
Green olives	3 ½ oz / 100 gr
Capers	1 tablespoon, chopped
Oregano	a pinch
Flour	½ cup / 100 gr
Fresh flat leaf parsley	1-2 tablespoons, chopped

1. Ask your fishmonger to scale and clean the fish for you.
2. Rinse the fish in cold water and patting them dry, dredge them in the flour, patting them with the palms of your hands to make the flour adhere.
3. Prepare the sauce: sauté the garlic in e.v.o.o. and, when it just turns golden, add the tomato, olives, capers and oregano. Cook, uncovered and stirring occasionally, over medium heat for 30 minutes.
4. Fry the fish in the e.v.o.o. until they've formed a nice golden crust on both sides.
5. Remove to a a platter covered with paper towel to absorb any excess oil.
6. Arrange the fish in a baking dish just big enough to accomodate them.
7. Pour the sauce over the fish.
8. Bake at 400°F/200°C/Gas Mark 6 for 15 minutes.
9. Serve hot.

SUGGESTED WINES:
Capri Bianco DOC - Campania
Campi Flegrei Falanghina DOC - Campania

TONNO ALLA CALABRESE
Tuna alla Calabrese

Fresh tuna steaks	1 ¾ lb / 800 gr
Extra virgin olive oil	¾ cup / 150 cc
Dry white wine	1 cup / 200 cc
White wine vinegar	2 teaspoons
Onion	1, thinly sliced
Flour	2 tablespoons
Tomato filets	1 ½ cups / 250 cc
Fresh flat leaf parsley	1 tablespoon
Bay leaf	4 leaves
Capers	1 tablespoon: washed, rinsed and chopped
Salte	to taste

1. Sear the tuna steaks in the e.v.o.o. over a high flame. When a crust has formed on the steaks, remove and set aside.
2. In the same oil, sauté the onion. When it's become transparent and begins to take a color, sift in the flour and, stirring, pour in the vinegar and the wine.
3. Reduce the sauce. When it becomes creamy, add the tomato filets, salt and bay leaves.
4. Return the steaks to the pan, cover with the sauce and cook over low heat for 8 minutes minutes.
5. Using a spatula, carefully turn over the steaks, add the parsley and capers, continue to cook for another few minutes.
6. Remove from the heat, allow to rest for a minute or two, then serve hot.

SUGGESTED WINES:
Donnici Rosato DOC - Calabria
Scavigna Bianco DOC - Calabria

TORTINO DI ALICI
Fresh Anchovy Torte

Fresh anchovies	2 ¼ lb / 1 kg
Bread crumbs	1 cup / 200 gr
Flour	1 cup / 200 gr
Fresh flat leaf parsley	2 tablespoons, finely chopped
Eggs	3
Garlic	3 cloves, chopped
Salt	to taste
Extra virgin olive oil	as needed

1. Clean the fish or have your fishmonger clean them for you – removing the heads, scaling and butterflying them.
2. Beat the eggs with the garlic, parsley and a pinch of salt.
3. Spread a generous layer of breadcrumbs on the bottom of a small baking dish, just large enough to accomodate the fish.
4. Dredge the butterflied fish in the flour, dip in the egg and arrange them, snuggly, in two layers over the breadcrumbs.
5. Cover abundantly with bread crumbs.
6. Arrange another two layers of breaded fish.
7. Cover abundantly with bread crumbs.
8. Drizzle with the e.v.o.o. then bake at 350°F/180°C/Gas Mark 4 for 30 minutes or until a crispy golden crust has formed on top.

SUGGESTED WINES:

Capri Bianco DOC - Campania
Castel del Monte Sauvignon DOC - Puglia

VITELLO ALLA PIZZAIOLA
Veal alla Pizzaiola

Veal cutlets - 8 cutlets	1 ¾ lb / 800 gr
Extra virgin olive oil	¼ cup / 50 cc
Garlic	2 cloves, thinly sliced
Tomato purée	2 cups / 400 cc
Oregano	1 tablespoon
Dry white wine	¼ cup / 50 cc
Salt and pepper	to taste

1. Quickly brown the cutlets on both sides in a frying pan with just enough e.v.o.o.
2. Remove to a warm platter.
3. Cook the tomato purée along with the e.v.o.o., garlic, oregano and wine.
4. Return the cutlets to the sauce when it is halfway done. After about 2 minutes, turn the cutlets over, add salt and pepper. Cook another few 2 minutes and serve hot with the sauce spooned over the cutlets.

SUGGESTED WINES:

Falerno del Massico Rosso Riserva DOC - Campania
Aglianico del Vulture DOC - Basilicata

IN THE KITCHEN

Various

Unless otherwise indicated, the recipes are for 4-6 people

ARANCINI DI RISOTTO AI PORCINI
Porcini Risotto Arancini

Leftover risotto? This is what to do with it! Delicious, quick and versatile!

1. Using your left over risotto (recipes on pg. 149 and 152), mix in grated parmigiano to taste, freshly ground pepper, and 2 or 3 eggs – quantities of these ingredients depend on the amount of left over risotto you have. You should have a nicely consistent mixture. If it's too loose, add in some breadcrumbs.
2. Use your hands to form the rice into balls more or less the size of a small orange, or if you prefer, into little loaves.
3. Roll the rice balls in bread crumbs.
4. Fry the balls 3-4 at a time in abundant e.v.o.o.
5. Use a spatula or slotted spoon to gently turn the balls so that they brown evenly on all sides.
6. Serve hot or at room temperature, accompanied by a fresh green salad.

SUGGESTED WINE:
Cori Rosso DOC - Lazio

ASPARAGI CON LE UOVA SODE
Asparagus with Hard Boiled Eggs

Thin fresh asparagus	2 ¼ lb / 1 kg
Hard boiled eggs	4, chopped
Extra virgin olive oil	as needed
Salt and pepper	to taste

1. Break off the hard base of each aspragus. This can be done easily by bending the spear-where it snaps is where the hard part separates from the tender part.
2. Cook the asparagus for 5-8 minutes, depending on how al dente you like them, in just enough boiling salted water to cover them.
3. Drain and rinse in cold water to stop the cooking process. Allow to dry.
4. Dress with e.v.o.o. and salt to taste.
5. Arrange the asparagus on a platter, in the form of a fan, with the base of the spears at the bottom.
6. Arrange the chopped hard boiled eggs at the base of the "fan", dusting them with freshly ground black pepper and drizzling with e.v.o.o.

BIGNÈ CON GAMBERETTI
Bigné with Shrimp

Puff pastry, see recipe on page 75	
Salt and pepper	to taste
Boiled shrimp	30-40 small, cleaned and chopped
Chopped fresh flat leaf parsley	as you like
Mayonaisse	4-5 heaping tablespoons

1. Cover the bottom of a baking pan or a cookie sheet with a sheet of parchment paper.
2. Place small dots of puff pastry batter about the size of a demi-tasse spoon on the parchment paper. Leave enough room between them because they will double in size as they bake.
3. Bake at 350°F/180°C/Gas Mark 4 for 10 minutes. Remove from the oven and allow to cool.
4. Mix all the other ingredients together.
5. Cut the puffs in half horizontally and, using a spoon, stuff them with the shrimp mixture.
6. Form a pyramid of puffs on a serving platter by putting a small dot of mayonaisse under the bottom of each puff so that it will adhere to the puff underneath.

SUGGESTED WINE:
Greco di Tufo (white) - Campania

BRIOCHE RUSTICA DI MARCELLA
Marcella's Savory Brioche

From the recipe of my cousin, Marcella Cioffi

Flour	2 cups/500 gr
Butter	½ cup/100 gr, melted then allowed to cool
Yeast	4 teaspoons/25 gr
Eggs	4
Milk	½ cup/100 cc
Salt and pepper	to taste
Sugar	2 tablespoons
Grated parmigiano	3 tablespoons
Boiled ham	5 ⅓ oz/150 gr, thickly sliced and diced
Sweet provolone cheese	3 ¼ oz/100 gr
Baby peas	7 oz/200 gr, cooked and dusted with flour

1. Warm the milk and put it into a mixing bowl with the yeast, a pinch of salt and a pinch of sugar.
2. When foam has formed on the surface of the milk, add the flour and all the other ingredients.
3. Mix well.
4. Cover the bowl with a cloth and put in a warm place for 2-3 hours.
5. Grease and dust with flour a ring pan.
6. Delicately pour the dough into the pan. This operation will deflate it a bit so return the pan to the warm location until the dough has grown again.
7. When the dough grows to the edge of the pan, place it on the bottom shelf of an oven that's been preheated to 350°F/180°C/Gas Mark 4 for 40 minutes.
8. Remove from the oven, allow to cool for 10 minutes, then turn over onto a cooling rack and allow to continue to cool.
9. Serve warm.

SUGGESTED WINE:
Lacryma Christi del Vesuvio Biano o Rosso DOC - Campania

CAMEMBERT IN SFOGLIA
Camembert in a Pastry Crust

Camembert or Brie	one 4"/10 cm round
Prepared puff pastry or filo-one pack, or see recipe on page 82	
Honey, mustard, jam	as you like
Egg yolk	1, mixed with 1 teaspoon water

1. Spread the pastry dough on your work surface and place the cheese in the center.
2. Spread the top of the cheese with whichever you prefer: honey, mustard, fruit preserve, jam, truffles.
3. Trim the pastry dough so that you can envelope the cheese, enclosing it inside the dough. Retain the excess dough.
4. Cut the excess dough into strips and use them to decorate the wrapped cheese.
5. Brush the surface with the egg yolk dilluted with water. This will form a lustrous glaze when baked.
6. Bake at 400°F/200°C/Gas Mark 6 for 20 minutes or until the crust is golden.
7. Remove from the oven and allow to cool for 10 minutes before serving.

CARCIOFI ALLA GIUDIA
Artichokes Jewish Style

"Romaneschi" (globe) artichokes	8
Extra virgin olive oil	as needed to fry the artichokes
Salt and pepper	to taste

1. Peel and clean the stems, leaving at least a few inches/centimeters. Cut 1/2-1"/1-2 cm off the top of the globes so that the artichokes will stand up in the pan.
2. Soak the artichokes in icy water for 30 minutes. Drain and dry completely.
3. Heat the oil in a medium size saucepan. There should be at least 1"/2 cm of oil in the pan, and it should be very hot.
4. Place the artichokes in the hot oil, stem facing up. As the artichokes open like flowers as they fry, press down on each one to make it open even more. Lower the heat, cover and cook for 15 minutes.
5. Remove the artichokes to a platter lined with several layers of paper towels to absorb the excess oil.
6. Delicately transfer the artichokes to a serving dish and serve, hot, sprinkled with salt and pepper.

- Use your fingers to eat the artichoke, one petal at a time, eating only the tenderest parts. Once all the petals are gone, sprinkle the heart with a little more salt and pepper and enjoy.

CAVOLFIORE IN CAMICIA
Cauliflower "in Camicia"

Cauliflower	1 large
Flour	1 cup/250 gr
Extra virgin olive oil	¼ cup/50 cc
Yeast	2 ¼ teaspoons/1 packet
Oil for frying	2 ½ cups/500 cc
Grated parmigiano	¼ cup/50 gr
Salt and pepper	to taste

1. Boil the cauliflower in salted water. Remove and drain when it is very al dente.
2. Break the cauliflower into pieces about the size of a walnut.
3. Prepare the batter: dissolve the yeast in a little warm water, add to it a pinch of salt and a teaspoon of e.v.o.o. Mix well until the yeast has completely dissolved, then mix in the flour.
4. Heat the frying oil in a deep pan. When the oil is very hot, dip the cauliflower pieces in the batter then fry them over high heat. Don't put too many pieces in the pan at once. When they begin to turn golden, lower the heat so they'll cook through.
5. When the cauliflower pieces are nice and golden, remove them from the oil using a slotted spoon or skimmer and lay them on paper towels to absorb the excess oil.
6. When all the cauliflower is cooked, arrange them on a platter and serve them sprinkled with grated parmigiano, salt and pepper.

SUGGESTED WINE:
Bolgheri Bianco DOC - Toscana

CIAMBOTTA

From the recipe of my cousin, Marcella Cioffi

Potatoes	2 ¼ lb / 1 kg, sliced into wedges
Red peppers	1 ¼ lb / 600 gr, sliced
Eggplants	1 ¼ lb / 600 gr, in large cubes
Extra virgin olive oil	2 cups / 500 cc
Peeled tomatoes	1 lb / 500 gr can, diced
Garlic	2 cloves, chopped
Fresh basil	3 tablespoons, chopped
Hot chili pepper	to taste
Salt	to taste

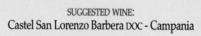

1. Fry the potatoes in abundant hot oil. Don't fry them all at once, or they won't be crisp. As they are done, remove them to a dish lined with paper towels to absorb the excess oil.
2. When the potatoes are all fried, fry the peppers. Remove to a paper towel lined dish.
3. Repeat with the eggplants.
4. Pour off the oil, leaving just enough to cover the bottom of the pan and brown the garlic and the chili pepper.
5. When the garlic begins to turn golden, add the tomatoes and the salt.
6. Cook over medium heat for about 10 minutes, then return the fried vegetables to the pan.
7. Reduce the heat, add the basil.
8. Turn off the heat, mix well and serve warm, or allow to cool and serve at room temperature.

SUGGESTED WINE:
Castel San Lorenzo Barbera DOC - Campania

CIPOLLE GRATINATE
Onions Gratin

Large round onions	2 lb/1 kg, sliced ½"/1 cm thick	Gaeta olives	½ cup/100 gr pitted
Salted anchovies	8 filets	Breadcrumbs	½ cup/100 gr
Capers	¼ cup/50 gr	Extra virgin olive oil	½ cup /100 cc

1. Pour ¼"/½ cm of hot water into a baking dish.
2. Arrange the onion slices in the baking dishes filling up the spaces between the larger slices with the smaller slices so that the onions are snugly packed.
3. Distribute the anchovies in pieces, the capers washed of their salt and the olives broken in half over all the onion slices.
4. Drizzle the oil over everything and sprkinkle with the breadcrumbs.
5. Bake the onions at 350°F/180°C/Gas Mark 4 on the lowest level of the oven for 15 minutes. When all the water will have evaporated, move the onions to the top level and continue baking until a golden crust forms over all.

- These onions are delicious served with puré of potatoes or as a side dish to accompany fried meatballs or cutlets.

SUGGESTED WINE:
Prosecco di Valdobbiadene DOCG - Veneto

CIPOLLE IN AGRODOLCE
Sweet and Sour Onions

Small white onions	1 lb/500 gr
Extra virgin olive oil	4 tablespoons
White wine vinegar	2 tablespoons
Sugar	2 tablespoons
Salt	to taste
Water	1 cup/200 cc

1. Put all the ingredients together in a medium sized pot or saucepan and cook, covered, for 30 minutes.
2. Uncover and continue to cook, stirring, until all the liquid has reduced to a thick nut-colored syrup.
3. The onions should be nicely golden-pay attention not to let them burn!
4. Serve the onions warm or room temperature.

COPPETTE DI PATATE CON CARNE
Potato Cups with Meat Filling

Yukon Gold Potatoes	8, all the same size
Rich béchamel	1 qt/1 lt, see recipe on page 66
Lean ground beef	¾ lb/300 gr
Prosciutto	3 ½ oz/100 gr, sliced into thin strips
Fontina cheese	3 ½ gr/100 gr, cubed
Dried porcini mushrooms	¼ cup/50 gr
Extra virgin olive oil	¼ cup/50 cc
Dry white wine	½ cup/100 cc
Fresh flat leaf parsley	1 tablespoon, chopped
Salt and pepper	to taste
Grated parmigiano	as needed
Bread crumbs	as needed

1. Soak the dried porcini mushrooms in warm water. When they are tender, drain, squeeze dry and chop.
2. Cut the potatoes in half and, using a spoon, scoop out a little cup in each half.
3. Slice a bit off the bottom of each potato half so that it will stand upright in the pan without flipping over.
4. Brown the ground beef in a little e.v.o.o. along with the mushrooms, salt, pepper and parsley.
5. Mix the rich béchamel with fontina and the meat.
6. Fill the potato cups with the meat mixture.
7. Cover the bottom of a baking dish with a little water, then arrange the potato cups in the dish.
8. Sprinkle all with grated parmigiano, breadcrumbs and pepper.
9. Bake at 350°F/180°C/Gas Mark 4 for 40 minutes or until a golden crust has formed.

SUGGESTED WINE:
Torgiano Bianco DOC - Umbria

CROSTONI AGLI ASPARAGI
Crostoni with Asparagus

A crostone is a thick slice of toasted bread topped with a variety of spreads or vegetables - a very popular appetizer everywhere in Italy

Slightly stale bread, sliced	½"/1 cm thick, toasted
Garlic	4 cloves
Extra virgin olive oil	4 tablespoons
Salt and pepper	to taste

1. Toast the sliced bread.
2. Steam or boil the asparagus al dente, then sauté in e.v.o.o. with the chopped garlic.
3. Lower the heat, add salt to taste and cook, covered, for 10 minutes.
4. Uncover, raise the heat and reduce the liquids.
5. Use an immersion blender to purée the asparagus. If you don't have an immersion blender you can simply chop the asparagus very finely.
6. Spread the asparagus on the crostoni and serve.

SUGGESTED WINE:
Greco di Tufo Bianco DOCG - Campania

CROSTONI AI CARCIOFI
Crostoni with Artichokes

8 slices of slightly stale bread, sliced	½"/1 cm thick, toasted as above
Artichokes	1 lb/500 gr, cleaned of all but their most tender leaves and leaving the stem
Garlic	2 cloves, chopped
Extra virgin olive oil	4 tablespoons
Salt and pepper	to taste
Fresh flat leaf parsley	as needed

1. Toast the bread.
2. Cut the artichokes into small pieces and steam or boil them until tender.
3. Drain, then sauté in the e.v.o.o. with the garlic.
4. Blend the cooked artichokes into a purée.
5. Spread on the toasted bread, and sprinkle with parsley before serving.

Con i carciofi è preferibile bere solo acqua

CROSTONI ALLE MELANZANE
Crostoni with Eggplant

8 slices of day-old bread, as on the previous page

Eggplants	1 lb / 500 gr
Garlic	2 cloves, chopped
Extra virgin olive oil	4 tablespoons
Salt and pepper or hot chili pepper	to taste
Fresh flat leaf parsley	as needed

1. Toast the bread and rub with the garlic cloves.
2. Peel the eggplants and cut into small cubes.
3. Sauté in the e.v.o.o. along with the garlic and pepper or hot chili pepper.
4. Add salt.
5. Cook, covered, for 15 minutes, stirring occasionally.
6. Uncover and continue to cook, allowing all the liquids to evaporate.
7. Purée the eggplants and spread on the slices of toasted bread.
8. Sprinkle with parsley before serving.

SUGGESTED WINE:
Primitivo di Manduria DOC - Puglia

CROSTONI AI FUNGHI
Crostoni with Mushrooms

8 slices of day-old bread bread, as on the previous page

Chiodini or other mushrooms	1 lb / 500 gr
Garlic	4 cloves, chopped
Extra virgin olive oil	4 tablespoons
Salt and pepper or hot chili pepper	to taste
Fresh flat leaf parsley	as needed

1. Toast the bread.
2. Wash the mushrooms then place in a pan with the e.v.o.o., garlic, salt, pepper or chili peppers.
3. Cook, covered, over medium heat for 15 minutes, stirring occasionally.
4. Uncover and continue cooking until the liquids reduce.
5. Finely chop the mushrooms then
6. Spread on the slices of toasted bread.
7. Sprinkle with parsley before serving.

SUGGESTED WINE:
Elogio di Casamonti I.G.T. - Toscana

ESCALIVADA DI JUANA
Juana Matilla Martinez' Escalivada

From the recipe of Eugene's mother

Red bell peppers	2
Yellow onions	2 large
Eggplants	2
Extra virgin olive oil	¼ cup / 50 cc
Fresh flat leaf parsley	2 tablespoons, chopped
Garlic	4 cloves, sliced or chopped
Salt	to taste

1. Bake all of the vegetables, whole, at 350°F/180°C/Gas Mark 4 for about 40 minutes.
2. When the eggplants' skin becomes charred and black, remove the vegetables from the oven and place in a paper bag. Fold the bag over to close the vegetables in it. This will make peeling the vegetables easier.
3. When they've cooled and are easy to handle, peel the vegetables.
4. Remove the seeds from the peppers and cut them into strips..
5. Cut the eggplant into strips.
6. Cut the onions into quarters.
7. Arrange the vegetables in their groups on a large serving platter.
8. When they have cooled to room temperature, sprinkle with the garlic, salt and parsley.
9. Drizzle with the e.v.o.o.

FAGIOLI E SCAROLA
Beans and Escarole

Cannellini beans	1 lb/500 gr, cooked and drained
Fresh escarole	2 lb/1 kg
Garlic	3 cloves, chopped
Extra virgin olive oil	½ cup/100 cc
Salt and pepper or hot chili pepper	to taste
Bruschetta (toasted bread) rubbed with garlic and drizzled with e.v.o.o.	as you like

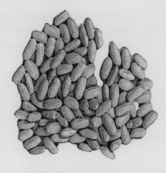

1. Soak the beans for 12 hours then boil for one hour.
2. Sauté the garlic in a pan with the e.v.o.o., along with the hot chili pepper (optional)
3. Coarsely chop the escarole and wash well. Without draining too well, transfer the escarole to the pan with the garlic.
4. Add salt, stir well over medium flame for a few minutes.
5. Cover, lower the flame and cook for 5 minutes.
6. Uncover, increadse the heat and sauté for another 5 minutes.
7. Serve hot, accompanied by the bruschette.

SUGGESTED WINE:
Montecarlo Bianco DOC - Toscana

FINOCCHI GRATINATI
Fennel Gratin

Fresh fennel	2 lb/1 kg
Grated parmigiano	½ cup/100 gr
Béchamel	1 qt/1 lt (see recipe on page 66)

1. Prepare the béchamel according to the recipe on page 66.
2. Clean the fennel, removing all but the tender parts. Cut into four, six or eight slices depending on the size of the fennel.
3. Steam until tender.
4. Allow to cool, dry using paper towels being careful not to break the fennel slices.
5. Arrange the fennel in a greased baking dish, then pour the béchamel over all.
6. Sprinkle the top with the grated parmigiano.
7. Bake at 350°F/180°C/Gas Mark 4 for 30 minutes or until a nice golden crust has formed.
8. Serve hot.

FRITTATA DI CIPOLLE
Onion Frittata

Large fresh eggs	8, beaten	Grated parmigiano	¼ cup/50 gr
Salt and pepper	to taste	Extra virgin olive oil	as needed
Onions (thinly sliced)	2 lb/1 kg,		

1. Sauté the onions in the e.v.o.o. in a large skillet.
2. Add salt, mix well, lower the heat and cover.
3. When the onions are cooked, uncover, raise the heat and continue to sauté for about 10 minutes until nicely caramelized.
4. Remove from the pan with a slotted spoon to a plate covered with paper towels to absorb any excess oil.
5. Beat the eggs together with the grated parmigiano. Mix the onions with the eggs and pour into the skillet with just enough e.v.o.o. to cover the bottom. Cook the frittata over medium heat for a few minutes, then lower the heat, cover, and continue cooking for another few minutes until the bottom has become nicely golden.
6. Flip over by holding the cover snuggly over the skillet and turning the skillet upside down over it, then sliding the overturned frittata back into the skillet.
7. Cook over medium heat for a few minutes until the bottom is golden.
8. Remove from the heat, cover and allow to rest for 15 minutes. Serve warm or at room temperature.

SUGGESTED WINE:
Greco di Tufo Bianco DOCG - Campania

FRITTATA DI PATATE
Potato Frittata

Large fresh eggs	8	Potatoes	2 lb / 1 kg
Extra virgin olive oil	as needed	Salt and pepper	to taste

1. Cube or thinly slice the potatoes.
2. Fry the potatoes in small batches and drain them on paper towels to absorb any excess oil.
3. When all the potatoes are fried, add them to the beaten eggs along with the salt and pepper.
4. Pour into a hot skillet with enough e.v.o.o. to cover the bottom and proceed as above.

SUGGESTED WINE:
Greco di Tufo Bianco DOCG - Campania

FRITTATA DI ASPARAGI O SPINACI
Asparagus or Spinach Frittata
Use only the tenderest part of very thin asparagus

Large fresh eggs	8
Salt and pepper	to taste
Extra virgin olive oil	¼ cup/50 cc
Asparagus or spinach	2 lb/1 kg
Grated parmigiano	¼ cup/50 gr

1. Steam the asparagus or spinach.
2. When tender, sauté briefly in e.v.o.o. with salt and pepper.
3. Beat the eggs together with the grated parmigiano.
4. Add the asparagus or spinach.
5. Continue to cook the frittata as on the previous page.

SUGGESTED WINE:
Greco di Tufo Bianco DOCG - Campania

FRITTATA DI CARCIOFI
Artichoke Frittata

Large fresh eggs	8
Extra virgin olive oil	as needed
Artichokes	2 lb/1 kg, cleaned of all but the tendest leaves and thinly sliced
Salt and pepper	to taste

1. Sauté the sliced artichokes in the e.v.o.o. until they are tender, without browning them.
2. Beat the eggs, mix in the artichokes, salt and pepper.
3. Continue to cook the frittata as on the previous page.

With artichokes, it's preferable to drink only water.

FRITTATINE CON MORTADELLA RICOTTA E SPINACI
Little crepes with Mortadella, or Ricotta and Spinach

Eggs	8
Milk	½ cup/100 cc
Flour	3 tablespoons
Salt and pepper	to taste
Mortadella	7 oz/200 gr, thinly sliced
Ricotta	¾ cup/200 gr
Spinach	¾ cup/7 oz/200 gr, sautée and chopped
Grated parmigiano	¼ cup/50 gr
Tomato sauce	½ qt/½ lt (see recipe on page 81)

1. Mix together the eggs, milk and flour.
2. Add a pinch of salt and pepper.
3. In a non-stick pan with a thread of e.v.o.o. use this batter to make little crepes.
4. Prepare the filling: mix together the spinach, ricotta, parmigiano, salt and pepper.
5. On half of the crepes, lay a slice of mortadella. Loosely roll the crepes up on themselves and arrange them in a baking dish in which you've spread a little tomato sauce.
6. Spread a spoonful or two of the ricotta mixture on the other half of the crepes, roll them up, being sure to not let the filling squeeze out the ends, and arrange them in the baking dish.
7. Cover each rolled up crepe with a little tomato sauce. To distinguish between the two fillings, you can put a little piece of mortadella on top of each the crepes that are filled with mortadella.
8. Bake at 350°F/180°C/Gas Mark 4 for 30 minutes.
9. Serve hot.

SUGGESTED WINE:
Lacryma Christi del Vesuvio Bianco o Rosso DOC - Campania

FRITTO MISTO

Potato purée	2 cups/1 lb/500 gr, already prepared	Egg whites	2
Cauliflower florets	1 lb / 500 gr	Bread crumbs	1/3 cup / 100 gr
Artichoke hearts	1 lb / 500 gr	Grated parmigiano	1/4 cup / 50 gr
Mozzarella, chilled, drained dry and cubed	¾ cup/7 oz/200 gr	The juice of half a lemon	
		Flour and olive oil for frying	as needed
		Salt and pepper	to taste
Eggs	4	Lettuce leaves	as needed

THE CROQUETTES

- Mix the potato purée with an egg, the grated parmigiano, salt and pepper. Taking a spoonful, shape into little balls or croquettes. Dredge in flour, dip in the egg white that's been lightly beaten, then dust them with breadcrumbs. Fry in hot olive oil until golden and crip on all sides.

THE CAULIFLOWER

- Steam the cauliflower until just tender. Prepare a light batter with the a beaten egg, a little flour, salt and pepper. Dip the florets in the batter then fry them in hot olive oil until they are golden and tender. You can check that they're done by piercing them with a fork.

THE ARTICHOKE HEARTS

- It's best to use artichokes that are not spiney. Remove all the tough leaves without pity! When you've gotten down to the tenderest leaves, cut the artichokes into four, six or 3 eight sections, depending on their size, and put them into a bowl that's been filled with cold water and a squeeze of fresh lemon juice. When all the artichokes are cleaned and sliced, drain and dry them well, prepare a batter as you did for the cauliflower and dip the artichokes in it before frying them in hot olive oil. Only fry a few artichokes at a time, turning them over so that they become golden and crisp on all sides. When they are done, place them on a paper towel to absorb any excess oil.

THE MOZZARELLA

- Dust the mozzarella cubes (make sure they're very cold!) with flour, dip them in the beaten egg and roll them in the breadcrumbs. Fry the cubes in hot olive oil a few at at time until they are golden and crisp. Don't fry too long, otherwise the mozzarella will melt! Sprinkle with salt.Salarli leggermente.

Arrange the lettuce leaves on a platter, then the fried vegetables and mozzarella over the lettuce and serve hot.

FUNGHI AL TONNO
Mushrooms with Tuna

Champignon mushroom caps	12 large
Tuna in olive oil, drained	14 oz/400 gr, crumbled
Onion	1, finely chopped
Garlic	2 cloves, finely chopped
Day old bread with the crusts removed	7 oz/200 gr, soaked in water then squeezed dry
Bread crumbs	¼ cup/50 gr
Dry white wine	¼ cup/50 cc
Fresh flat-leaf parsley	2 tablespoons, chopped
Extra virgin olive oil	4 teaspoons/20 cc
Curry powder	a pinch
Salt and pepper	to taste

1. Sauté the onion and garlic in the e.v.o.o. When they start to become golden, add the curry and the tuna.
2. Cook for a few minutes, stirring occasionally. Add the wine.
3. When the wine has reduced, transfer everything into a mixing bowl and mix it with the bread, parsley, salt and pepper.
4. Fill the mushroom caps with the tuna mixture, and place snugly, them into a baking pan.
5. Sprinkle with breadcrumbs.
6. Pour a half glass of water into the baking dish, drizzle the stuffed mushroom caps with e.v.o.o.
7. Bake at 400°F/200°C/Gas Mark 6 for 30 minutes.

SUGGESTED WINE:
Orvieto Bianco DOC - Umbria

FUNGHI ALLO SPECK
Mushrooms with Speck

Use only the tenderest part of very thin asparagus

Champignon mushroom caps	12 large
Speck, or similar smoked ham	10 ½ oz 300 gr
Fontina cheese	7 oz/200 gr, in tiny cubes
Day old bread with the crusts removed	10 ½ oz/300 gr, soaked in water then squeezed dry
Grated parmigiano	⅓ cup/100 gr
Eggs	2
Extra virgin olive oil	4 teaspoons/20 cc
Salt and pepper	to taste

1. Mix the bread with the speck, the fontina, half the grated parmigiano, the eggs, salt and pepper.
2. Stuff the mushroom caps with this mixture.
3. Arrange the mushroom caps in a greased baking pan.
4. Pour a half glass of water into the bottom of the pan.
5. Sprinkle with the rest of the grated parmigiano and bake at 400°F/200°C/Gas Mark 6 for 30 minutes.

SUGGESTED WINE:
Lago di Caldaro Classico DOC (red) - Trentino Alto Adige

GATTÒ DI PATATE A "MODO MIO"
Potato Pie "My way"

Potatoes	2 lb / 1 kg
Boiled ham	7 oz / 100 gr, cut into small pieces or strips
Provola (smoked mozzarella)	7 oz / 200 gr, in small cubes
Grated parmigiano	½ cup / 100gr
Bread crumbs	¼ cup / 50 gr
Hard boiled eggs	4, sliced
Milk	2 cups / ½ liter
Heavy cream	2 cups / ½ liter
Butter	¾ cup / 150 gr
Salt and pepper	to taste

1. Boil the potatoes, peel then purée them.
2. Cook the puréed potatoes with the milk, heavy cream, butter, salt and pepper until it becomes velvety.
3. Grease a baking dish with butter and sprinkle it with some of the breadcrumbs.
4. Fill the baking dish with 2/3 of the potato purée.
5. Arrange the provola, prosciutto and hard boiled eggs over the purée.
6. Cover with the remaining purée, sprinkle with the rest of the bread crumbs, grated parmigiano and dots of butter.
7. Bake at 400°F / 200° C / Gas Mark 6 for 40 minutes, until a golden crust has formed over the top.
8. Serve hot.

SUGGESTED WINE:
Cortese di Gavi DOCG - Piemonte

INSALATA RUSSA
"Russian" Potato Salad

Mayonaisse	1 cup/200 gr
Potatoes	2 medium, cubed
Carrots	3 medium, diced
Zucchini	3 tender and small
Green beans	3 ½ oz/100 gr, cut into small pieces
Green peas	¾ cup/100 gr
Salt and pepper	to taste

1. Boil the vegetables. When they are al dente, cool them under running cold water.
2. Dry and salt them, then mix them with the mayonaisse.
3. If you like, you can use a mold of your choosing to give the salad a shape!
4. Refrigerate for several hours, then turn it over (if it's been held in a mold) onto a serving platter.
5. You can use this "russian salad" to stuff nice, firm, ripe round tomatoes that have had their "caps" removed and their seeds scooped out.

SUGGESTED WINE:
Lacryma Christi del Vesuvio Bianco DOC - Campania
Vernaccia di San Gimignano DOCG - Toscana

MEDAGLIONI
DI MELANZANE E PEPERONI
Eggplant and Pepper Medallions

Large globe eggplants	2
Red bell peppers	2
Mozzarella	7 oz/200 gr, sliced
Flour	½ cup/100 gr
Egg	2, beaten
Extra virgin olive oil	½ cup/100 cc
Garlic	2 cloves, chopped and 2 cloves whole
Tomato purée	1 ½ cups/300 gr
Grated parmigiano	¼cup/50 gr
Oregano, salt and pepper	to taste
Bread	8 thick slices

1. Slice the eggplants about 1/2"/1 cm thick.
2. Place the eggplant slices, a few at a time, in a large non-stick pan over medium heat to "dry" them. The heat will evaporate some of the eggplant's water content, rendering them more tender.
3. Dredge the slices in flour, pressing with your fingers to adhere the flour to the eggplant.
4. Dip the slices in the beaten egg, then fry them in the e.v.o.o. Set aside.
5. Roast, then peel the peppers.
6. After removing their seeds, cut them into thick slices. Drizzle with a little e.v.o.o. and lightly salt them.
7. Arrange half of the eggplant in a baking pan, leaving room between the slices.
8. Place a slice of mozzarella on each slice.
9. Sprinkle all with oregano, salt and pepper.
10. Cover with another slice of eggplant and another slice of mozzarella.
11. Sprinkle again with oregano, salt and pepper.
12. Spoon the tomato sauce over the eggplant.
13. Arrange two slices in an "X" on the top of each eggplant medallion.
14. Another slice of mozzarella and a spoon of tomato sauce.
15. Sprinkle all with the grated parmigiano.
16. Bake at 400°F/200°C/Gas mark 6 for about 20 minutes.
17. Cut the sliced bread into discs slightly larger than the eggplant slices, being sure to eliminate any crust. Grill the discs and rub them with the whole garlic cloves.
18. Serve each eggplant medallion on a bread disc.

SUGGESTED WINE:
Castel del Monte Sauvignon Bianco - Puglia

MELANZANE ALLA PIZZAIOLA
Eggplant alla Pizzaiola

Italian eggplants, all of the same size	8
Tomato filets	14 oz/400gr, diced
Extra virgin olive oil	½ cup/100 cc
Oregano	1 tablespoons
Garlic	4 cloves, sliced
Salt and pepper	to taste

1. Cut the eggplants in half, lengthwise.
2. Using a sharp knife, score a criss-cross pattern in the exposed meat of each egg-plant half.
3. Arrange the eggplants snuggly in a baking dish. Spoon the diced tomato over them, sprinkle with salt, pepper, garlic and oregano.
4. Drizzle the e.v.o.o. over all.
5. Bake at 350°F/180°C/Gas Mark 4 for 40 minutes.
6. Remove from the oven and allow to rest before serving.
7. The eggplants are delicious hot or at room temperature.

SUGGESTED WINE:
Santa Margherita di Belice Nero d'Avola DOC - Sicilia

MELANZANE CON RISO E CARNE
Eggplants with Rice and Meat

Long "Italian" eggplants	8, all the same size
Rice	1 cup/200 gr
Ground beef	7 oz/200 gr
Extra virgin olive oil	½ cup/100 cc
Onion	1, finely diced
Eggs	2
Fresh flat leaf parsley	2 tablespoons, chopped
Garlic	1 clove, chopped
Tomato purée	1 ¼ cup/250 cc
Mozzarella	1 ¾ cup/200 gr, cubed
Grated parmigiano	½ cup/100 gr
Salt and pepper	to taste

1. Cook the rice in salted water. When it is al dente, rinse it under cold water to stop the cooking process.
2. Cut the eggplants lengthwise and, using a spoon, scoop out a trench in the center leaving the walls rather thick. Chop the pulp that you've scooped out of the eggplants and set aside.
3. Sauté the eggplant halves in the e.v.o.o. until they're almost cooked, being sure not to burn them.
4. Arrange the eggplant halves in a baking dish.
5. Drain most of the excess oil from the frying pan. Sauté the onion and garlic. When the onion becomes glossy, add the chopped eggplant pulp and the meat. Cook over medium heat, mixing and breaking it apart with a fork.
6. Add salt to taste and a few spoonsful of tomato purée which will have been reduced slightly in a saucepan.
7. In a mixing bowl, combine the rice, the eggs, part of the parmigiano, salt and pepper. Mix well, add the cooked meat and blend it in with the rice. Distribute this stuffing over the eggplant halves.
8. Cover with the tomato sauce, sprinkle with the rest of the parmigiano and a little pepper. Drizzle with a little e.v.o.o.
9. Bake at 400°F/200°C/Gas Mark 6 for 20 minutes.
10. Remove and allow to cool before serving.

SUGGESTED WINE:
Lacryma Christi del Vesuvio Rosso DOC - Campania

PANE PUGLIESE
Pugliese Bread

Flour	1 ½ cups/300gr
Powdered yeast	½ teaspoon/3gr
Warm water	6 tablespoons
Cold water	¾ cup/150cc

1. Put the warm water in a large mixing bowl along with the yeast. When the yeast has dissolved thoroughly, add the cold water.
2. Mix well until you obtain a small loaf.
3. Place the bowl in a warm place and allow it to rest for 24 hours.

FOR THE BREAD:

Duram wheat flour	1 ½ cups/300gr
All purpose flour	1 ¼ cups/250gr
Water	¾ cup/300cc
Yeast	2 teaspoons/10gr
Egg yolks	2
Salt	4 teaspoons/20 gr

1. Use 1 cup/9 oz/250 gr of the mother yeast.
2. Dissolve the yeast in a little warm water, then mix in the two types of flour and the egg yolks.
3. Add the water and salt, and begin to knead.
4. Knead the dough thoroughly, turning it frequently.
5. Allow the dough to rest for 10 minutes.
6. Spread it out on your work surface, then roll it up on itself.
7. Place the dough in a warm place and let rest for about 2 hours. When it has doubled in size, place it in a greased pan and bake at 450°F/240°C/Gas Mark 8 for 40 minutes.
8. Remove from the oven and allow to cool before slicing.

- The bread is especially delicious when you break it apart with your hands while it's still warm, rather than slicing it!

- Fantastic spread with herb butter or any soft, spreadable cheese.

PANE DI GENZANO
Genzano-style Bread

FOR THE MOTHER YEAST:

Flour	4 ½ cups / 450 gr
Powdered yeast	1 teaspoon / 5 gr
Cold water	½ cup / 150cc

1. Put the warm water in a large mixing bowl along with the yeast. When the yeast has dissolved thoroughly, add the cold water.
2. Mix well until you obtain a small loaf.
3. Place the bowl in a warm place and allow it to rest for 24 hours.

FOR THE BREAD:

Flour	5 cups / 500 gr
Water	2 cups / 500 cc
Yeast	1 ½ teaspoons / 10gr
Egg yolks	2
Salt	4 teaspoons / 20 gr

1. Heat the water to about 86°F / 30°C.
2. Crumble the yeast into the wate and stir until it's well dissolved.
3. Add the mother yeast.
4. Mix well, add the flour and salt.
5. Knead very well, turning the dough frequently, until it has an even consitency.
6. Put the loaf, covered, in a warm place and allow it to rise until it has doubled in size.
7. Put the dough on a pan or sheet and bake at 450°F / 240°C / Gas Mark 8 for 45 minutes.
8. If you'd like to give the loaf a more regular shape, you can bake it in a round baking dish or in a loaf pan.

- When the bead has cooled it can be sliced, or you can break it apart with your hands while it's still warm! Delicious with any soft cheese or with herb butter.

PANZANELLA
Tuscan Bread Salad

Stale bread	1 lb/500 gr
Ripe tomatoes	3 large and firm, cut into small pieces
Onion	1, chopped
Basil	2 tablespoons, coarsley chopped
White wine vinegar	1 tablespoon
Extra virgin olive oil	¼ cup/50 cc
Salt and pepper	to taste

1. Soak the bread briefly in water, squeeze it dry and break it apart with your hands into a mixing bowl.
2. Mix in the tomato and onion.
3. Add the salt, pepper, basil, vinegar and e.v.o.o.
4. Mix well and allow to rest for at least a half hour before serving.

SUGGESTED WINE:
Vernaccia di San Gimignano DOCG - Toscana

PARMIGIANA DI MELANZANE
Eggplant parmigiana

*The name of this legendary dish refers to the Northern city of Parma
but its origins are firmly planted in Naples! Today it is probably one of the most well
known and loved Italian dishes in the world.
We present it in its most authentic neopolitan form.*

Long Italian eggplants	4
All purpose flour	as needed
Eggs	3
Tomato purée	2 cups/500 cc
Fresh basil	to taste
Extra virgin olive oil	as needed for frying
Mozzarella	10 ½ oz/300 gr
Eggs	4, hard boiled
Grated Parmigiano	to taste
Salt and pepper	to taste

1. Dust the sliced eggplant in flour, dip them in the beaten egg and fry in hot oil, turning them, until golden brown. Set aside.
2. Cook the tomato purée with a pinch of salt until it is moderately dense.
3. Spoon a little of the tomato sauce onto the bottom of a baking dish and spread it out to cover.
4. Arrange a layer of fried eggplant in the pan being careful to cover the entire bottom of the pan.
5. Spoon a little sauce over the eggplant.
6. Arrange slices of mozzarella and sliced hard boiled egg over the eggplant. Cover with grated parmigiano, pepper, fresh basil leaves and more tomato sauce.
7. Arrange another layer of fried eggplant in the pan, covering it with tomato sauce and abundant grated parmigiano.
8. Bake in an oven preheated to 375°F/180°C/Gas Mark 4 for 45 minutes, making sure that the top becomes crispy but not dry.
9. Remove from the oven and allow to rest. Serve luke-warm.

SUGGESTED WINE:
Aglianico del Taburno DOCG - Campania

PAPPA AL POMODORO
Tuscan Bread and Tomato Soup

Vegetable broth	2 cups / 500 cc (see recipe on page 67)
Extra virgin olive oil	1/4 cup / 50 cc
Peeled plum tomatoes	2 cups / 500 gr, drained and chopped.
Day old bread	1 lb / 500 gr, cubed
Fresh basil	2 tablespoons, chopped and 20 whole leaves
Garlic	3 cloves, sliced
Salt and pepper or hot chili pepper	to taste

1. Sauté the garlic in the e.v.o.o.. Just as it begins to turn golden, add the tomatoes and chopped basil, and cook over high heat for about 15 minutes.
2. Add the bread. Spoon in the hot broth as needed to achieve the consistency of a thick potage.
3. Mix in the salt and pepper or hot chili pepper to taste.
4. Cook together for another 15 minutes or so, then remove from the heat and allow to rest for 15 minutes.
5. Serve hot, decorating each bowl with a few basil leaves.

SUGGESTED WINE:
Chianti Classico Casamonti DOCG - Toscana

PEPERONI AL TONNO
Peppers Stuffed with Tuna

Red bell peppers	8 small and meaty
Tuna in olive oil, drained	2 cups/450 gr
Day old bread with the crusts removed	2 cups/450 gr
Breadcrumbs	½ cup/100 gr
Grated parmigiano	¼ cup/50 gr
Gaeta olives	1 cup/200 gr, pitted
Salted capers	⅓ to ½ cup/80 gr
Salted anchovies	4
Extra virgin olive oil	½ cup/100 cc
Pepper	to taste

1. In a mixing bowl, crumble the tuna with a fork.
2. Soak the bread in water, squeeze dry then crumble it into the bowl with the tuna.
3. Rinse the capers and anchovies in warm water to remove their salt.
4. Coarsely chop the olives, capers and anchovies and add them to the tuna.
5. Add the bread crumbs, the parmigiano, pepper and e.v.o.o.
6. Cut the cap off each pepper and carefully remove its seeds . Fill them with the tuna stuffing, packing it snugly.
7. Cover each pepper with its cap. Arrange the peppers tightly in a baking dish just big enough to hold them.
8. Pour about 1"/2 ½ cm of water mixed with a little bit of e.v.o.o. and a pinch of salt into the baking dish.
9. Bake at 350°F/180°C/Gas Mark 4 for 45-60 minutes.
10. Remove from the oven and allow to cool. Serve at room temperature.

SUGGESTED WINE:
Greco di Tufo DOCG - Campania

PEPERONI CON RISO E CARNE
Peppers Stuffed Rice and Meat

Red bell peppers	8 all the same size
Ground beef	7 oz/200 gr
Rice	¾ cup/300 gr, cooked and cooled
Eggs	2
Onion	1, chopped
Garlic	1 clove, chopped
Fresh flat leaf parsley	1 tablespoon, chopped
Extra virgin olive oil	¼ cup/50 cc
Grated parmigiano	¼ cup/50 gr
Tomato paste	2 tablespoons
Dry white wine	¼ cup/50 cc

1. Sauté the onion and garlic in e.v.o.o.
2. Add the ground beef, crumbling it with a fork.
3. Dissolve the tomato paste in the wine and add it to the meat.
4. When the meat has browned nicely, transfer it to a large mixing bowl and combine it with the rice, parmigiano, the eggs and parsley.
5. Cut the caps off the peppers and carely remove their seeds.
6. Fill each pepper snugly with the stuffing. Cover the peppers with their caps and arrange them tightly in a baking dish into which you will pour about 1"/2 ¼ cm of water.
7. Bake at 400°F/200°C/Gas Mark 6 for 30-40 minutes.
8. Serve warm.

SUGGESTED WINE:
Lacryma Christi del Vesuvio Rosso DOC - Campania

PIZZA DI SCAROLA
Stuffed Pizza with Escarole

Pasta for pizza (see recipe on page 81)	1 lb/500 gr
Escarole	1 lb/500 kg
Salted anchovies	6 filets, washed, dried and chopped
Capers	¼ cup/50 gr, chopped
Gaeta olives	½ cup/100 gr, chopped
Garlic	4 cloves, thinly sliced
Extra virgin olive oil to fry in	2 ½ cups/500 cc

1. Wash and chop the escarole.
2. Sauté the garlic and escarole in the e.v.o.o.
3. Add the olives, capers and anchovies and continue to sauté.
4. When the escarole is tender, remove from the heat and allow to cool.
5. Divide the pizza dough into two. Roll one part out into a disc with a diameter of about 14"/35 cm.
6. Grease a round 12" 30 cm baking pan with sides about 1"/3 cm high.
7. Lay the disc into the pan, covering also its sides.
8. Distribute the escarole evenly over the dough.
9. Roll the other half of the dough out into a disc the same as the first, and cover the pan with it. Using a knife, trim off the excess dough.
10. Use the tines of a fork to press down the border of the dough all around the pan, then use the fork to perforate the top of the pizza.
11. Bake at 400°F/200°C/Gas Mark 6 for 30 minutes.
12. Remove and allow to cool. The pizza should be served tepid or at room temperture.

SUGGESTED WINE:
Copertino Rosato DOC - Puglia

PIZZELLE FRITTE DI ORSOLA
Fried Pizzelle

From the recipe of my cousin, Orsola Lonigo Latour

All Purpose Flour	1 ½ cup/250gr
Potatoes	3 ½ oz/100gr, boiled, peeled and riced
Egg yolk	1
Warm milk	¼ cup/50cc
Yeast	1 packet
Simple tomato sauce (see recipe on page 81)	1 ½ cup/250cc
Mozzarella	3 ½ oz/100gr
Basil	10 leaves
Extra virgin olive oil	2 ½ cups/500 cc
Salt and pepper	to taste

1. Dissolive the yeast in the warm milk with a pinch of salt.
2. On your work surface, form the flour into a "volcano". When the yeast has become foamy on the surface, pour it into the "crater" and mix it into the flour.
3. Add the riced potato, milk, egg and a salt.
4. Mix well.
5. Form the dough into a loaf and put it aside to grow for about one hour.
6. Roll the dough out to a sheet about 1/2" / 1 cm thick then use the bottom of a glass like a cookie cutter to cut out rounds of dough. Use a glass with the diameter that you prefer!
7. As you cut out the rounds of dough, place them on a cloth that's been lightly dusted with flour.
8. Cover with another cloth and allow to rise for at least 30 minutes.
9. Heat the e.v.o.o. and when it is very hot, fry the pizza rounds, turning them to brown them on both sides.
10. As they become nicely golden, remove them to a warmed platter.
11. While the pizzette fry, prepare a simple tomato sauce by cooking tomato purée with a pinch of salt and a tablespoon of e.v.o.o.
12. Spoon some sauce over the pizzette as they are placed on the serving platter.
13. On each pizzetta place a slice of mozzarella and a leaf of basil.
14. Serve hot!

SUGGESTED WINE:
Lacryma Christi del Vesuvio Rosso DOC - Campania

PIZZELLE CON LA SCAROLA
Pizzelle with Escarole

Pizza dough (see recipe on page 81)	9 oz/250 gr
Escarole	1 lb/500 gr, washed and chopped
Salted anchovies	6 filets, washed, dried and chopped
Salted capers	¼ cup/50 gr, washed of their salt and chopped
Gaeta olvives	½ cup/100 gr, pitted and chopped
Garlic	4 cloves, thinly sliced
Extra virgin olive oil	2 ½ cups/500cc

1. Prepare the pizza dough according to the recipe on page 81.
2. Form the dough into a loaf and put it aside to grow for about two hours.
3. In the meantime, sauté the garlic and escarole in e.v.o.o.
4. Add the olives, capers and anchovies.
5. Dust your work surface with flour and roll out the dough to a thickness of about 1/4″ / 1/2 cm.
6. Use a glass with a diameter of about 2 1/2″ / 6-7 cm to cut out discs of pizza dough. Leave them on the work surface, cover them with a dry cloth and let them rest for about 30 minutes.
7. Place a spoonful of escarole filling on each disc then fold the disc over to form a "half moon".
8. Using a fork, press down along their edges, sealing the edges of the pizzelle.
9. Fry the pizzelle in abundant hot e.v.o.o., 4 or 5 at a time, basting them with the hot oil as they fry.
10. The pizzelle will inflate – at this point you can turn them over to brown on the other side.
11. When they are golden brown, remove them with a slotted spoon and place them on paper towel to absorb the excess oil.
12. Serve hot!

SUGGESTED WINE:
Lacryma Christi del Vesuvio Rosso DOC - Campania

POMMES DAUPHINE

An elegant version of the potato croquette, they can accompany scaloppine,
stewed meats or be part of a "fritto misto"

Potato purèe	2 1/2 cups / 500 gr
Bigné dough (see page 75)	1 lb / 500 gr

POTATO PURÉE:	
Potatoes	1 lb / 500 gr
Butter	¼ cup / 50 gr
Whole milk	½ cup / 100 cc
Salt	to taste
Extra virgin olive oil	as needed to fry the pommes dauphine

1. Boil the potatoes, peel them and mash them using a potato masher.
2. Cook the potatoes together with the butter, milk and salt.
3. Stir continuously so that the purée won't stick to the pan and until the milk has been completely absorbed. Allow to cool until it is tepid.
4. Mix the potato purée with the bigné dough.
5. Using two spoons, form quenelles about the size of a walnut and drop them into the hot the hot e.v.o.o.
6. Fry the pommes dauphine, a few at a time, turning them over once or twice until they are evenly golden. When they are done, rest them on paper towels to absorb the excess oil.
7. Serve hot.

SUGGESTED WINE:
Soave Superiore DOCG (bianco) - Veneto

PROVOLA IN CARROZZA
Smoked Mozzarella "in Carrozza"

Bread	20 slices ½″/1 cm thick, with the crusts removed
Provola (smoked mozzarella)	10 slices, kept refrigerated for at least two days
Salted anchovy filets	20, washed in warm water to deprive them of their salt
Milk	½ cup/100 cc
Eggs	4, beaten
Flour	1 cup/200 gr
Extra virgin olive oil	1 cup/200 cc

1. Cover the bottom of a tray or baking pan with the flour, then arrange 10 slices of bread over it.
2. Wet the bread with milk.
3. Put a slice of provola on each slice, and two anchovy filets over each slice of provola.
4. Wet the remaining slices of bread with milk and cover the first 10 to form sandwiches.
5. Dust the sandwiches abundantly with flour.
6. Picking up each sandwich one by one, shake off any excess flour, dip in the egg on both sides and place it delicately in a frying pan with the hot e.v.o.o.
7. Turn the sandwich over repeatedly until it is beautifully golden on both sides.
8. Serve piping hot.

SUGGESTED WINE:
Sant'Agata dei Goti Rosato DOC - Campania

RAMEQUINS DI ANGELICA
Angelica's Ramaquins

Little bignets with cheese, prosciutto or zucchini flowers.
From the recipe of Angelica Alfani Latour

Water	1 ¼ cup/250 gr
Butter	¼ cup/100 gr
All Purpose Flour	1 ½ cups/150 gr
Medium eggs	4
Salt	a pinch
Fontina cheese	3 ½ oz/100 gr
or	
Lean prosciutto	3 ½ oz/100 gr
or	
Zucchini flowers	10, finely chopped
Extra virgin olive oil	1 qt/1 liter

1. Bring the water to the boil with a pinch of salt. When it boils, add the butter.
2. When the butter has melted, add the flour all at once.
3. Stir continuously until the batter no longer sticks to the sides of the pot.
4. Stir a few more seconds, then transfer the batter to a large mixing bowl.
5. Spread the batter out in the bowl so that it cools quickly.
6. When it has reached room temperature, mix in one egg at a time incorporating the eggs well into the batter.
7. Add the fontina, the prosciutto or the squash blossoms and gently mix into the batter. Or... divide the batter into a thirds and mix in each of the three ingredients!
8. Heat the oil medium-high in a medium size pot. The oil should be at least 2"/5 cm deep.
9. Using two teaspoons, take a little ball of batter and carefully place it into the hot oil. Keep adding little balls of batter to the hot oil, leaving enough space for them to puff up.
10. As they cook, the ramaquins will turn over by themselves several times.
11. Lower the flame, allowing the ramaquins to cook inside. When they become golden and fluffy, raise the heat to high. This will draw the oil out of them so that they will not be greasy.
12. Remove them from the oil using a slotted spoon and allow to drain on a sheet of absorbant paper. Serve hot!

- Ramaquins are wonderful as an antipasto, an aperitivo (cocktail) or as a side.

SUGGESTED WINE:
Spumante Marchese Antinori Nature - Veneto e Trentino

STRUDEL DI CIPOLLE
Onion Strudel

Flaky puff pastry	(see recipe on page 82)
Yellow onions	1 lb / 500 gr, thinly sliced
Eggs	4
Emmenthal (swiss cheese)	7 oz / 200 gr, sliced
Grated parmigiano	¼ cup / 50 gr
Breadcrumbs	¼ cup / 50 gr
Egg yolk	1, lightly beaten with a teaspoon of water
Extra virgin olive oil	½ cup / 100 cc
Salt and pepper	to taste

1. Sauté the onions in the e.v.o.o. in a large pan, stirring and tossing frequently, until they are nicely caramelized.
2. Use a slotted spoon to remove them to a platter lined with paper towel to absorb the excess oil.
3. Beat the eggs with salt and pepper to taste. Add a tablespoon of parmigiano and mix in the onions.
4. Make a frittata in a frying pan with a little e.v.o.o., cooking it, covered, over medium heat. When its surface begins to become solid, flip it over and cook it on the other side. To do this, hold the cover firmly onto the pan and flip the pan upside down. Hold the cover, upside down with the frittata on it and gently slip it back into the pan.
5. Roll out the pastry dough and lay it into a baking dish lined with parchment paper.
6. Arrange the slices of cheese on the dough, leaving a border free all around.
7. Lay the frittata over the cheese. If you need to, you can fold it in half so that it fits just over the the cheese..
8. Fold the dough over the frittata, closing it like an envelope.
9. Turn it over delicately on the parchment paper so that the seam remains on the bottom.
10. Brush the top with the beaten egg yolk.
11. Sprinkle with the bread crumbs and the rest of the parmigiano.
12. Bake at 400°F / 200°C / Gas Mark 6 for 30 minutes.
13. Remove from the oven and allow to cool. Serve warm or at room temperature.

SUGGESTED WINE:
Cirò Bianco - Calabria

UOVA ALLA MONACHINA
Eggs in the style of the "Little Nun"

A very typical neapolitan antipasto

Eggs	10
Egg whites	2, beaten
Bèchamel sauce (see page 66)	2 ½ cups / 500 cc
Flour	¾ cup / 125 gr
Bread crumbs	½ cup / 100 gr
Extra virgin olive oil	2 ½ cups / 500 cc
Salt and pepper	to taste

1. Hard boil the eggs and allow them to cool.
2. Prepare a dense béchamel according to the recipe on page 66. Allow it to cool.
3. Cut the hard boiled eggs in half lengthwise, remove the yolks to a mixing bowl and crumble them with a fork. Mix them with the bèchamel along with a pinch of salt and pepper. Refrigerate for a couple of hours.
4. Holding an egg half in one hand, place a spoonful of egg yolk-béchamel in the yolk's cavity. Roll it in your hands to give it the form of a whole egg. Repeat this step with all of the egg halves.
5. Roll the eggs in flour, dip them in the beaten egg whites then roll them in the bread crumbs being sure to cover each egg uniformly.
6. Fry the eggs a few at a time in the hot e.v.o.o. When they've become golden on one side, carefully turn them over with a fork and spoon to brown them on the other side.
7. As they are done, lay them on a paper towel to absorb any excess oil.
8. Serve hot, accompanied by asparagus, artichokes or green peas.

SUGGESTED WINE:
Cirò Bianco - Calabria

ZUCCHINE ALLA SCAPECE
Fried Pickled Zucchini with Mint

Small, tender zucchini	2 lbs/1 kg
Vegetable oil	2 ½ cups/500 cc
Extra virgin olive oil	1/4 cup/50 cc
White wine vinegar	3 tablespoons
Garlic	2 cloves, thinly sliced
Salt and pepper	to taste
Fresh mint leaves	2 tablespoons, chopped

1. Slice the zucchini into rounds no more than 1/4" / 1/2 cm thick.
2. Fry them in the vegetable oil a few at a time until almost crisp.
3. As they are fried, remove them to a platter covered with paper towel to absorb any excess oil.
4. When all the zucchini are fried, put them in a deep bowl, drizzle them with the e.v.o.o. and mix them with the vinegar, garlic, salt, pepper and mint. Press down on the zucchini with the back of a spoon in order that they soak up all the condiment.
5. Cover with plastic wrap and allow them to rest for two days before serving at room temperature.
6. Do not refrigerate.

SUGGESTED WINE:
*Because of the major role that vinegar plays in any "scapeche" recipes,
wine is not recommended as an ideal beverage accompaniment.*

ZUPPA DI FAGIOLI
Bean Soup

Borlotti beans	2 ½ cups / 500 gr, soaked overnight, cooked 1 hour and drained.
If borlotti are not available, you can use pinto, cranberry or kidney beans.	
Peeled plum tomatoes	½ cup / 100 gr, chopped
Garlic	2 cloves, finely chopped
Sage	6-8 leaves
Rosemary	a sprig, fresh or 1 tablespoon dried
Extra virgin olive oil	as you like
Salt	to taste

1. Sauté the garlic in the e.v.o.o. in a saucepan or pot.
2. When the garlic becomes glossy, add the sage and rosemary and allow the oil to infuse with their aromas. After a few minutes, add the tomatoes and cook to reduce.
3. Add the beans to the pot along with some of their broth and let them cook, uncovered, for 15 minutes.
4. As the broth reduces to you liking, add salt to taste.
5. Serve the soup with toasted bread and, if you like, grilled sausages.

SUGGESTED WINE:
Morellino di Scansano DOCG - Toscana

ZUPPETTA DI FIORILLI
Zucchine Flowers Soup

Zucchine flowers	1 cup / 200 gr, chopped	
Small, tender baby zucchine	1 lb / 500 gr	
New potatoes	2 ½ cups / 500 gr, cubed	
Extra virgin olive oil	¼ cup / 50 gr	
Garlic	2 cloves, whole	
Salt and pepper or hot chili pepper	to taste	

1. Sauté the garlic in the e.v.o.o. in a saucepan or pot. When they are nicely golden, remove them from the pot.
2. Add the zucchine flowers , the zucchine and the potatoes to the pot.
3. Sauté them for a few minutes, cover with water. Bring the water to a boil then lower it to a brisk simmer for about 10 minutes.
4. Add salt and pepper or chili pepper to taste to taste.

• Serve with toasted bread rubbed with fresh garlic and drizzled with e.v.o.o.

SUGGESTED WINE:
Ischia Bianco - Campania

In the kitchen

Desserts

BABÀ

All purpose or Manitoba flour	1 lb/500 gr
Milk	1 cup/250 cc
Dry active yeast	one packet
Butter	melted and cooled - ¾ cup/150 gr
Sugar	⅓ cup/60 gr
Eggs	3, large
The zest of one organic lemon	
Salt	a pinch

1. Mix together in the bowl of a kitchen mixer: the yeast, a little warm milk, the salt and a tablespoon of sugar. As soon as the mix begins to foam (about 20 minutes), add in the other ingredients.
2. Use the mixer's hook attachment to mix the batter at medium speed for 30 minutes. The batter will no longer stick to the sides of the bowl. At this point, you can proceed to fill the ring mold - fill it only halfway.
3. Put the mold in a warm place and let the babà rise until it has reached the level of the mold's rim.
4. Preheat the oven to 350°F/180°C/Gas Mark 4. Place the babà on a grill that's been positioned on the floor of the oven and bake for 45 minutes.
5. Remove from the oven and let cool for 15 minutes, then turn it over onto a deep serving dish.
6. When the babà has completely cooled, pour the syrup over it, soaking it completely.
7. To serve the babà, slice it, plate it, drizzle a little straight rum over each slice as well as a generous spoonful of pastry cream and a dollop of cherry preserve.

FOR THE SYRUP	
Water	1 qt/1 lt
Sugar	1 ¾ cups/350 gr
The zest of 1 organic lemon	
Dark rum	1 ½ cups / 350 cc

1. Boil the water together with the sugar, lemon zest. Add half the rum and keep boiling kfor 10 minutes to evaporate the alcohol.
2. Remove from the heat and let cool before using.

- If you don't have a kitchen mixer with a hook attachment, you can achieve the same results beating the batter by hand for one hour. The babà can be made in individual cylindrical molds - fill each mold to ⅓, let rise until the batter reaches the rim then bake at 350°F/180°C/Gas Mark 4 for 20 minutes.

CANTUCCI ALLE MANDORLE
Almond Biscotti

Cantucci are an ancient cookie that have been popular since the Renaissance.
They are best dipped in Vin Santo

Toasted almonds	3 ½ cups / 600 gr
All purpose flour	1 cup / 200 gr
Active dry yeast	2 teaspoons
Butter	½ cup / 100 gr
Sugar	2 cups / 400 gr
Eggs	6 whole + 4 whites

1. In a large bowl, mix together ⅓ of the whole toasted almonds, ⅓ of the toasted almonds chopped and the last ⅓ ground into flour.
2. Mix the flour with the yeast, sift it into the almonds. Melt the butter - when it's cooled mix it in with the almonds and flour. Mix in the sugar.
3. Beat the egg whites until stiff and blend them into the mixture with a spatula, along with the 6 whole eggs.
4. Form two loaves and bake in two 4x8" / 10x20 cm loaf pan at 350°F/180°C/Gas Mark 4 for 30 minutes.
5. Remove from the oven. When the loaves have cooled, cut them into ½" / 1 ½ cm slices. Return them to the oven to bake at 250°F/120°C Gas Mark ½ for 15 minutes.
6. Remove from the oven, let cool
7. Cantuccini can be stored in a sealed container for a long time.

- Instead of almonds, you can use toasted hazelnuts, pine nuts (pinoli), pistacchios, chocolate chips or candied orange.

SUGGESTED WINE:
Vin Santo di Montagliari - Toscana

CASTAGNACCIO

Chestnut flour	1 ½ cups/300 gr	Extra virgin olive oil	2 tablespoons, very warm
Sugar	1 ¼ tablespoon-15 gr	Rosemary	1 tablespoon
Warm water	as needed	Salt	to taste
Pine nuts (pinoli)	½ cup/50 gr		

1. Mix together the chestnut flour, sugar, salt and enough warm water to produce a rather thick, consistent batter.
2. If using fresh rosemary, remove the leaves from the stem - discard the stem. Infuse the rosemary in the warmed olive oil. Mix the rosemary with the pine nuts.
3. Lightly grease a shallow baking pan with e.v.o.o., then spread the batter evenly in the pan. The pan should be large enough so that the batter will be about 3/2″/2 cm high. Sprinkle the pine nuts and rosemary over the batter, press in with your hands.
4. Bake at 400°F/200°C/Gas Mark 6 for about 20 minutes, until the surface is golden. Cool before serving

SUGGESTED WINE:
Elba Aleatico Rosso - Toscana

GELATO AL VIN SANTO

Almond cantucci (biscotti)	16
Vin Santo	⅓ cup/100 cc
Custard gelato	see below

FOR THE GELATO:

Pastry cream	3 ½ cups/800 gr
Vin Santo	¼ cup/50 cc
Crushed toasted almonds	⅓ cup/100 gr

1. Blend the vin santo into the pastry cream.
2. Pour it into a gelato machine. If you don't have one, place the bowl of pastry cream in the freezer and stir it very frequently.
3. When the gelato is ready, pack it into a rectangular container that's been lined with plastic cling wrap. Return it to the freezer for a few hours.
4. To serve, arrange 4 cantucci, one next to the other, on each dish. Splash the cantucci with Vin Santo and let them soak it up for 10 minutes. Cut the gelato into slices and place a slice over the cantucci.
5. Decorate each slice of gelato sprinkling it with crushed toasted almonds.

CROSTATA DI MELE O CILIEGE
Apple of Cherry Tart

Shortbread (see recipe on page 78)	a disc 14"/35 cm wide
Pan di Spagna (see recipe on page 74)	a disc 12"/30 cm wide
Pastry cream (see recipe on page 69)	2 ½ cups/500 cc
Apples, sliced, or cherries, pitted	2 ½ cups/500 gr
Apricot jelly	2-3 tablespoons
Cane sugar	to taste
Cinnamon powder	as needed

1. Cut a 12"/30 cm parchment paper disc and place it on the bottom of a round 12"/30 cm baking pan.
2. Lay the shortbread disc into the pan, uniformly covering the bottom and about 3/4"/2 cm up the sides. Pierce the dough on the bottom with a fork.
3. Brush the dough with a generous amount of apricot jelly, then place the pan di spagna disc over it.
4. If you're using apples, arrange the slices over the pan di spagna, brush with a little more apricot jelly.
5. If you're using cherries, spread a layer of pastry cream over the pan di spagna, then arrange the pitted cherries over it.
6. Sprinkle with sugar and cinnamon.
7. Bake at 350°F/180°C/Gas Mark 4 for 35-40 minutes.
8. Allow to cool before serving.

SUGGESTED WINE:
Albana di Romagna Amabile DOCG - Emilia Romagna

DOLCE DI CASTAGNE
Chestnut Log

Chestnuts	3 lb/1 ½ kg
Unsweetened chocolate	7 oz/200 gr, grated
Sugar	½ cup/100 gr
Whole milk	2 cups/500 cc
Thick pastry cream (see recipe on page 69)	2 cups/500 cc
Coffee butter cream (see recipe on page 68)	1 ½ cups/300 gr
Bay leaves	2
Salt	a pinch
Unsweetened cocoa powder	as needed

1. After peeling the chestnuts, boil them in enough water to cover along with the bay leaves and a pinch of salt.
2. Test for doneness by piercing a chestnut with the tip of a sharp knife.
3. Drain the chestnuts and remove their skins. This is easier to do while the chestnuts are still hot.
4. Mash the chestnuts using a potato ricer while they are hot.
5. Put the mashed chestnuts into a pot along with the chocolate, sugar and milk, and cook over low heat until you obtain a dense purée.
6. Allow to cool
7. Spread the chestnut purée out on a clean cloth.
8. Spread another clean cloth over the chestnut purée. Using a rolling pin, roll it out into a rectangle about 1/2" / 1 cm thick.
9. Remove the top cloth, then spread the pastry cream evenly over the chestnut purée. Don't spread the cream all the way to the edges of the rectangle - in this way, the cream won't squeeze out when you roll the log.
10. Pick up the border of the cloth and delicately roll the chestnut up onto itself, forming a log. Wrap the log snugly in the cloth, tying the ends as if it were a giant bon-bon.
11. Refrigerate for a few hours. When the log is well chilled, carefully place it on a long serving platter. Cover it with the coffee buttercream.
12. Use a fork to etch lines along the surface of the buttercream, then sprinkle the log with the cocoa.
13. Keep refrigerated until you're ready to serve in thick slices. To cut the log, use a knife that's been dipped into hot water then dried.

SUGGESTED WINE:
Moscato di Siracusa Bianco - Sicilia
Lacryma Christi del Vesuvio Liquoroso Bianco - Campania

MADDALENE
Madeleines

*La Madeleine - the small shell-shaped cake that sent Marcel Proust into
reveries of remembrance of times past... enjoy them warm from the oven,
dunked in tea, hot chocolate, caffè latte - any time, anywhere.
They last a week or two stored in a tin - if you and your family can resist!*

Sugar	1 ¼ cups/250 gr
Butter	1 cup/250 gr
Egg yolks	1 cup/250 gr - about 12 large
All Purpose Flour	2 ¼ cup/225 gr
Powdered Yeast	1 level teaspoon (a little less than one packet)/5 gr

1. Melt the butter. Allow to cool to room temperature.
2. In a large mixing bowl, delicately mix together the sugar and the egg yolks.
3. Mix the flour with the yeast and sift into the sugar/egg mixture.
4. Add the melted butter.
5. Cover the bowl and refrigerate for at least 3 or 4 hours.
6. Grease the maddalene pan. This is a baking pan with (usually) 12 shell-shaped forms or molds. The pan can be made of aluminum, non-stick-coated metal, silicone or other material. I like the aluminum best - not the non-stick type. The pan is most easily greased using the spray shortening that you prefer.
7. Fill the molds with batter. The easiest and most reliable way to do this is to use a 1 ½″ 4 cm ice cream scoop - the kind with a spring-release to expel the batter from the scoop. Of course, you can use anything you like or have handy, but we've found (after lots and lots of maddalene) that this is our favorite method.
8. Bake in an oven preheated to 400°F/200° C/Gas Mark 6 for 12 minutes. When the maddalene are soft but firm to the touch, they're done.
9. Allow to cool about 10 minutes in the molds, then remove with the help of a blunt-tipped knife.
10. Optional: sprinkle with confectioners sugar before serving.

- The classic recipe for maddalene is as above. Enjoy them plain, as Proust did when he was a boy, with a cup of hot tea... or add lemon or orange zest, raisins, saffron, chopped almonds, hazlenuts, pistachios, or chocolate chips to the batter! Let your imagination loose!

SUGGESTED WINE:
Sauterne Château Romer - Francia

MONTEBIANCO

Chestnuts	2 lb/1 kg
Milk	1 qt/1 lt
Bay leaves	2
Salt	a pinch
Confectioners' sugar	½ cup/100 gr
Cocoa powder	¾ cup/150 gr
Whipped cream	2 ½ cups/500 cc
Heavy (double) cream	¼ cup/50 cc

1. Peel the chestnuts.
2. Boil the chestnuts in the milk along with the bay leaves and a pinch of salt.
3. Use a shart knife to pierce the chestnuts to test if they are done. When they are tender, drain and remove the brown skins while they're still hot.
4. Use a potato ricer to mash the chestnuts into a mixing bowl.
5. Mix in ½ cup/100 gr of the cocoa powder, the powdered sugar and the cream.
6. Cook over medium heat, stirring continuously, until you have a rather dry dough.
7. Using the potato ricer, extrude the chestnut dough onto a serving platter such that you create a little "mountain".
8. Fill a pastry (piping) bag with the whipped cream and elegantly decorate the chestnut mountain.
9. Dust with the remaining cocoa powder.
10. Refrigerate until you are ready to serve.

SUGGESTED WINE:
Greco di Bianco - Calabria

MOUSSE AL CIOCCOLATO
Chocolate Mousse

The recipe is from Signora Rosaria, the personal cook of
Umberto Agnelli who loved this dessert

Unsweetened chocolate	1 ½ cup/250 gr, finely grated
Heavy (double) cream	½ cup/100 cc
Egg yolks	6
Butter	1 ½ tablespoons/20 gr
Vanilla bean	1

1. Finely grate the chocolate in a food processor, then melt it in a double boiler or bain-marie.
2. Add the butter, allow to cool to room temperature.
3. Cut the vanilla bean lengthwise and using a knife, scrape the beans into the melted chocolate.
4. Add the egg yolks one at a time, stirring vigorously.
5. Whip the cream, then using a spatula, delicately fold it into the chocolate.
6. Refrigerate overnight.

- Serve the mousse in champagne glasses, decorated with milk chocolate shavings.

SUGGESTED WINE:
Lacryma Christi del Vesuvio Liquoroso Bianco - Campania
Vin Santo - Toscana

MOUSSE AL LIMONE
Lemon Mousse

This is a recipe of the Agnelli family - a gift from Signora Rosaria,
Umberto Agnelli's personal cook, to my mother

Organic lemons	5
Eggs	5
Sugar	½ cup / 90 gr
Unflavored gelatin	1 ½ sheets/¼ teaspoon/1 ¼ gr
Butter	¾ cup/150 gr
Lemon flavored shortbread cookies	as you like

1. Separate the eggs.
2. Using an electric mixer, blend the sugar and egg yolks over a double boiler or bain-marie.
3. Transfer the mixture to a bowl and continue to beat until it cools to room temperature.
4. Combine the juice of two of the lemons with the zest of all four lemons.
5. Add the gelatin.
6. Beat the egg whites until they are stiff, then gently fold them into the egg mixture.
7. Refrigerate for at least two hours.
8. To serve, place a spoonful of crumbled lemon shortbread biscuits into glass cups then fill with the lemon mousse. Serve well chilled.

SUGGESTED WINE:
Malvasia delle Lipari Bianco - Sicilia

OPERA

*This Viennese tart is one of the most delicate desserts you can offer
at the end of an elegant dinner.*

ALMOND GÉNOISE

Almond flour	1 ½ cups / 250 gr		Butter	3 tablespoons / 45 gr
Flour	3/4 cup / 70 gr		Eggs	
Powdered sugar	1 ¾ cups / 250 gr 6			

1. Use an electric mixer to beat together the sugar and eggs over a double boiler or bain-marie.
2. Remove from the heat and continue to beat the egg mixture, adding the butter, the flour and the almond flour.
3. Beat the egg whites until stiff, then gently fold them into the mixture.
4. Bake at 350°F / 180°C / Gas Mark 4 for 25 minutes in a low rectangular baking pan large enough to cut into 2 10" / 25 cm squares.

SYRUP

Water	1 cup / 250 cc	Strong expresso coffee	¼ cup / 50 cc,
Sugar	1 ⅓ cup / 150 gr	room temperature	

1. Bring the water to a boil, dissolve the sugar in it, then add the coffee.

COFFEE BUTTERCREAM

Vanilla	1 pod	Egg yolks	4
Butter	¾ cup / 150 gr	Strong espresso coffee	½ cup / 100 cc
Sugar	1 ⅓ cup / 150 gr		

1. Cut the vanilla bean in half and, using the knife, scrape the insides into a tablespoon of very hot water.
2. Whisk together the butter and sugar in a mixing bowl.
3. Whisk in the egg yolks, the coffee and the vanilla infused water.
4. Spread the buttercream evenly on the first génoise square, then cover with the second square.

GANACHE
(See recipe on page 69)

- Pour the ganache evenly over the entire surface of the cake. Allow the cake to rest overnight before serving it. Dip a sharp knife into very hot water, then wipe it dry before cutting each slice.

PASTIERA NAPOLETANA

Shortbread dough (see recipe on page 78)	2 lb/1 kg
Cooked wheat kernels	14 oz/400 gr
(available in jars in most groceries)	
Whole milk	¼ cup/50 cc
Ricotta	1 ¾ cups/14 oz/400 gr
Sugar	1 ½ cups/300 gr
Eggs	5
Orange blossom water	1 or 2 tablespoons
The zest of 1 organic lemon	
Candied fruit (orange and citron)	¼ cup/50 gr
Confectioners' sugar	as needed

1. Cook the wheat in the milk for 10 minutes, stirring frequently, until it takes on a creamy consistency. Allow to cool.
2. Pass the ricotta through a food mill into a large mixing bowl and combine it with the sugar, the egg yolks, the candied fruit, the lemon zest and the cooked wheat.
3. Some peole don't prefer to find large pieces of candied fruit in their pastiera, so if you like, you can pass the fruit through the food mill before adding it to the ricotta mixture.
4. Beat the egg whites until they're stiff, then fold them delicately into the ricotta mixture.
5. Roll the shortbread dough out to a disc slightly larger than the 12"/30 cm baking pan that you will use. Line the bottom and the sides of the pan with the dough.
6. Pour the ricotta mixture into the pie.
7. Cut the leftover dough into strips as wide as you like (you can use a zig-zag pastry wheel) and arrange them into a criss-cross pattern to decorate the top of the pie.
8. Bake at 350°F/180°C/Gas Mark 4 for 60 minutes on the bottom shelf of the oven.
9. Allow to cool, sprinkle with confectioners' sugar before serving.

- The pastiera is even more delicious the day after it's baked. Do not refrigerate!
- This pie is difficult to transfer to a serving dish, so be prepared to slice it in it's baking pan.

SUGGESTED WINE:
Sant'Agata dei Goti Falanghina Passito Bianco - Campania

PERE AL VINO DI GIANNINA
Giannina's Pears Baked in Red Wine

From the recipe of Giannina Alfani Lonigo

Kaiser pears	4, not too ripe
Marmelade or honey	8 tablespoons
Powdered cinnamon	to taste
Rosemary and bay leaves	to taste
Dry red wine	2 cups / 500 cc

1. Cut the pears in half and scoop out the seeds.
2. Place the herbs in a baking dish just large enough to hold the 8 pear halves snugly. Arrange the pears over the herbs.
3. Place a spoonful of marmelade or honey into the cavity where the seeds have been scooped out
4. Sprinkle the pears with cinnamon and pour the wine into the dish.
5. Bake at 350°F/180°C/Gas Mark 4 for about 45 minutes on the bottom shelf of the oven.
6. Check to make sure that the wine hasn't fully dried. By the time the pears are cooked the wine should have condensed into a thick syrup. Add more wine if necessary.
7. Allow to cool. Serve the pear halves with the wine sauce spooned over them.

- Serve at room temperature.

SACHER TORTE

This delicious Austrian torte is known and highly regarded in all the world.

Flour	2 cups/200 gr
Butter	¾ cup/200 gr
Sugar	1 cup/180 gr
Unsweetened chocolate	6 ½ oz/180 gr
Heavy (double) cream	¾ cup/180 cc
Eggs	6
Granular yeast	½ packet
Apricot jam	as needed

1. Mix the butter and sugar together.
2. Separate the eggs.
3. Incorporate the egg yolks into the butter, one yolk at a time.
4. Melt the chocolate in the cream over low-medium heat. When it's all melted, remove from the heat and allow to cool.
5. Add the chocolate cream to the butter, then sift in the flour.
6. Beat the egg whites until stiff and fold them delicately into the batter.
7. Pour the batter into a 12″/30 cm baking dish that has been greased and the bottom lined with parchment paper.
8. Bake at 350°F/180°C/Gas Mark 4 for 40 minutes.
9. Remove from the oven and allow to cool. When the cake is cool, turn it out, upside down, onto a cake dish.
10. Cut the cake in half horizontally. Spread the apricot marmelade, which has been warmed the passed through a sieve, on the bottom half. Cover with the other half, spread a thin layer of the same warmed, sieved marmelade. Pour a thin, even layer of the icing over the cake, repeat several times in order to have a nice, thick chocolate icing.

FOR THE ICING	
Hot water	3 tablespoons
Unsweetened chocolate	5 ½ oz/150 gr
Butter	2 tablespoons/30 gr
Confectioners' sugar	½ cup/100 gr

1. Melt the chocolate in a double boiler or bain-marie.
2. Mix in the butter, sugar and hot water.

SUGGESTED WINE:
Barolo Chinato Rosso - Piemonte

SBRISOLONA

The typical cake of the wonderful city of Mantova

All purpose flour	2 cups / 200 gr
Corn meal	½ cup / 100 gr
Granulated sugar	1 ½ cups / 300 gr
Almonds	1 cups / 150 gr, coarsly ground
Almonds	1 cup / 150 gr, finely ground
The zest of 1 organic lemon	
Salt	a pinch
Butter	1 ¾ cups / 200 gr, chilled and cubed
Eggs	4
Lemon juice	1 tablespoon
Bread crumbs	as needed

1. Mix together the two types of flour, the sugar and the almonds.
2. Add the butter and mix together until you have a very crumbly mixture.
3. Add the eggs, the lemon zest, lemon juice and salt.
4. Mix everything together but don't use your hands, which would warm the batter and melt the butter!
5. Grease a 12" / 30 cm baking pan and sprinkle it with bread crumbs.
6. Pour the crumbly batter into the pan, spreading it evenly. Bake at 375°F / 190°C / Gas Mark 5 for 40 minutes.
7. Allow to cool before serving. The sbrisolona can't be sliced - break it apart!

- A delicious variation is to mix into the batter 7 oz / 200 gr of chocolate broken into small pieces! You can use bitter, bittersweet or milk chocolate... or a little of each!

SUGGESTED WINE:
Albana di Romagna Amabile DOCG - Emilia Romagna

SCAZZETTA DI PANTALEONE

Pantaleone is the most historic pastry shop of Salerno. As I wrote in the 'tales', this is where all the 'buongustai', of the city would come for their pastries, including my great-grandparents, during the 1800's. The Scazzetta is the cake that Pantaleone is known for.

Génoise pastry dough (see recipe on page 79)	1 lb 5 oz / 600 gr
Pastry cream (see recipe on page 69)	1 lb / 500 gr
Wild (or very small cultivated) strawberries	1 ½ cups / 350 gr
Dry white wine	1 cup / 200 cc

FOR THE GLAZE

Wild (or very small cultivated) strawberries	2 ½ cups / 500 gr
Confectioners' sugar	3 ¾ cups / 500 gr

1. Cook the strawberries together with the sugar over medium heat. When the strawberries and the sugar have dissolved, render them into a dense syrup using an immersion blender.
2. Remove from heat and allow to cool

FOR THE SYRUP

Water	2 cups / 500 cc
Sugar	1 ⅓ cup / 250 gr
Maraschino, Strega or a liqueur of you choice	¼ cup / 50 cc

1. Slice the génoise cake horizontally into two layers.
2. Soak each half generously with the syrup.
3. Place the bottom half on a cake dish.
4. Spread the pastry cream evenly over the cake, then cover completely with the strawberries which will have been rinsed in the white wine and allowed to dry.
5. Cover with the other half of the génoise. Pour the warm glaze evenly over the entire cake, including the sides.
6. Decorate the cake all around its base with strawberries.

- Keep the cake refregerated. It will be even more delicious the day after you make it.

TORTA AI TRE CIOCCOLATI
Three-Chocolate Cake

CHOCOLATE PAN DI SPAGNA
(see recipe on page 74)

GIANDUJA CREAM FOR THE FILLING		GANACHE ICING	
Gianduja chocolate	7 oz/200 gr	Unsweetened chocolate	1⅓ cups/
Heavy (double) cream	1 cup/200 cc		10½ oz/300 gr
		Heavy (double) cream	¾ cup/200 cc

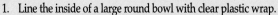

FOR THE SYRUP			
Water	1 qt/1 lt	Unsweetened cocoa	½ cup/100 gr
Sugar	2 ½ cups/500 gr	Cognac or rum	½ cup/100 cc
		Cocoa to cover	as needed

1. Line the inside of a large round bowl with clear plastic wrap.
2. Divide the pan di Spagna batter into three 12"/30 cm low cake pans and bake at 400°F/200°C/Gas Mark 6 for 20 minutes. Allow to cool, then thoroughly soak with the syrup, which has been prepared by boiling the water with all the syrup ingredients until the alcohol has evaporated.
3. Prepare the gianduja cream by simmering the gianduja chocolate in the heavy (double) cream. When the chocolate has completely melted and the cream become dense, remove from the heat and allow it to cool.
4. Spread half of the ganache, then place the middle layer over it. Soak the second pan di Spagna layer with syrup.
5. Spread the rest of the ganache over the second layer, then lay the third layer over it.
6. Soak the top layer with syrup and refrigerate the cake for a few hours.
7. For the ganache: bring the heavy (double) cream to a boil and melt the grated dark chocolate in it. Stir continuously until it becomes creamy and smooth. Pour the warm ganache over the cake, covering it evenly. Using a spatula, collect the ganache that has collected on the dish to spread it, evenly, on the cake.
8. When the ganache has cooled, use a small sifter to dust the cake with the cocoa.
9. Refrigerate until ready to serve.
10. Slice the cake with a sharp knife dipped in hot water then dried.

TORTA AI DUE CIOCCOLATI
Double Chocolate Cake

I tasted this cake during a visit to a delightful little town near Florence.
The owner of the pastry shop, touched by my pleas, gave me his recipe.

Pasta génoise	(see recipe on page 79)
Chocolate buttercream	(see recipe on page 68)
Ganache	(see recipe on page 69)
Sugar	¾ cup / 200 gr
Hot water	1 cup / 200 cc
"Strega" liqueur	¼ cup / 50 cc
Chocolate shavings	as needed

1. Prepare a syrup with the hot water, sugar and Strega.
2. Cut the génoise cake in half, horizontally, and soak both halves generously with the syrup.
3. Spread the chocolate buttercream, about ¼" / ½ cm thick, on the bottom génoise layer.
4. Cover with the other génoise half.
5. Pour the ganache over the cake, allowing it to cover the tops and sides evenly.
6. Cover the sides of the cake with chocolate shavings.
7. To slice the cake, dip a sharp knife into hot water and immediately dried with a towel. Repeat this process after cutting each slice.

SUGGESTED WINE:
Moscato di Pantelleria - Sicilia
Vin Santo - Toscana

TORTA CIOCCOLATO E NOCI DI FELICITA
Felicita's Chocolate and Walnut Cake

From the recipe of Felicita Latour.

All purpose flour	1 ½ cups / 300 gr
Cocoa powder	¾ cup / 150 gr
Raw sugar	1 ⅓ cups / 250 gr
Honey	⅓ cup / 100 gr
Butter	1 cup / 250 gr
Eggs	6, separated
Granulated yeast	2 packets
Chopped walnuts	2 cups / 250 gr
Confectioners sugar or cocoa to sprinkle over the cake	as needed

1. Using an electric mixer, beat together the sugar, honey and egg yolks over a double boiler or bain-marie.
2. When the mixture is smoothly blended, remove it from the heat and continue to mix in the flour, the cocoa and the yeast.
3. Melt the butter, allow it to cool then mix it, along with the crushed walnuts, with the flour mixture.
4. Beat the egg whites until they are stiff. Gently fold them into the batter.
5. Pour the batter into a greased cake pan that has been lined with parchment paper.
6. Bake for 45 minutes in an oven that's been preheated to 350°F / 180°C / Gas Mark 4. When you see tiny cracks begin to open on the cake's surface, it's ready to be removed from the oven and allowed to cool for 15 minutes before turning it over onto a serving dish.
7. When the cake has completely cooled, sprinkle it with confectioners sugar or powdered cocoa.

SUGGESTED WINE:
Aleatico di Gradoli Liquoroso Rosso - Lazio

TORTA CAPRESE CLASSICA

Almonds	3 ½ cups / 300 gr
Unsweetened chocolate	7 oz / 200 gr, grated
Unsalted butter	¾ cup / 200 gr, melted
Simple butterless biscuits, like "Social Teas"	10, crumbled
Medium whole eggs	5
Sugar	1 cup / 200 gr
Sliced almonds	½ cup / 100 gr

1. Finely chop 1 ¾ cup / 150 gr of the almonds in a food processor and set aside.
2. Place the other half of almonds along with the biscuits and the sugar in the processor and reduce to the consistency of flour.
3. Grind the unsweetened chocolate in the food processor.
4. Melt the butter. When it is all melted and very hot, mix in the ground chocolate.
5. In a mixing bowl, combine all the processed ingredients with the melted butter and chocolate.
6. Mix well, then add the eggs one at a time.
7. Grease a 12" / 30 cm baking tin and dust it with flour.
8. Cut a parchment paper disc to cover the base of the pan and grease it with butter.
9. Cover the bottom of the pan with the sliced almonds.
10. Pour the batter into the pan and bake on the bottom shelf of the oven at 400°F / 200°C / Gas Mark 6 for 30 minutes.
11. When it is cooked, remove from the oven, allow to cool before turning the cake over onto a serving dish.

TORTA CAPRESE AL LIMONE
Lemon Torta Caprese

- As above, but substitute the dark chocolate with white chocolate and add the zest of one organic lemon to the batter. Sprinkle with powdered sugar or shaved white chocolate.

SUGGESTED WINE:
Lacryma Christi del Vesuvio Liquoroso Bianco - Campania

TORTA CON L'INGANNO
Cake with a Trick

This cake is ready to trick you! With it's pure white exterior, it could even be a wedding cake... but when you slice it open... surprise!

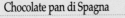

Chocolate pan di Spagna	see recipe on page 74

FOR THE SYRUP

Water	1 cup/250 cc
Sugar	4-5 tablespoons
Cocoa powder	3 heaping tablespoons
Cognac or other spirit	to taste

FOR THE GANACHE

Gianduja chocolate	7 oz/200 gr
Heavey (double) cream	1 cup/200 cc

FOR THE GANACHE ICING

White chocolate	7 oz/200 gr
Heavy (double) cream	½ cup/100 cc

Grated unsweetened coconut

1. Bake the pan di Spagna at 350°F/180°C/Gas Mark 4 for 20 minutes.
2. When it has cooled, cut it horizontally into three layers.
3. Put the bottom layer on a dish and soak it with syrup.
4. Spread half of the ganache, then place the middle layer over it. Soak the second pan di Spagna layer with syrup.
5. Spread the rest of the ganache over the second layer, then lay the third layer over it.
6. Soak the top layer with syrup and refrigerate the cake for a few hours.
7. When the cake is thoroughly chilled it can be frosted with the white ganache. Cover the top and sides evenly. Naturally, the ganache will have to be warmed slightly to make it fluid enough to flow easily over the cake.
8. After a few minutes, sprinkle the entire cake generously with the coconut, covering the tops and sides.
9. To slice the cake, dip a very sharp knife in hot water, wipe it quickly with a towel and cut. Repeat this for every two or three slices.

TORTA DEL SACRIPANTINO DI ANGELICA
Angelica's Sacripantino Cake

From the recipe of Angelica Alfani Latour

Génoise (see recipe on page 79)	
Unsweetened chocolate	7 oz/200 gr, grated
White chocolate	7 oz/200 gr, grated
Chocolate shavings	⅓ cup/100 gr
Heavy (double) cream	1 ½ cups/300 cc
Sugar	¾ cup/150 gr
Eggs	2 yolks
Flour	¼ cup/25 gr
Rum	¼ cup/50 cc
Marsala wine	¼ cup/50 cc

1. Prepare the génoise according to the recipe on page 79.
2. To avoid the problem of having to cut the génoise in two thin layers, you can divide the batter into two low cake tins.
3. For the syrup, boil 1 cup/200 cc of water with the sugar. When the sugar is completely dissolved, add all but a tablespoon each of the rum and the marsala. As soon as the syrup returns to a boil, remove it from the heat.
4. Prepare a pastry cream with ¼ cup/50 gr sugar, the 2 egg yolks and the flour mixed with the ½ cup/100 cc of the heavy (double) cream. Stir in the rest of the rum and marsala.
5. Stir the cream over medium heat and, when it has become smooth and dense, stir in the grated white chocolate.
6. Remove from the heat and allow to cool
7. Bring the rest of the heavy (double) cream to a boil. Add the grated unsweetened chocolate. Stir well. Remove from the heat but keep warm.
8. Place a layer of génoise on a platter. Uniformly spoon syrup over the cake.
9. Spread the white chocolate pastry cream over the génoise.
10. Soak the other layer of génoise with the rest of the syrup and delicately lay it over the white chocolate pastry cream.
11. Carefully pour the bitter chocolate cream over the entire surface of the cake, starting at the center and spiraling out toward the edges. Try to cover the sides of the cake, too, with the cream.
12. Decorate the cake with the shaved chocolate.
13. Refrigerate for at least one day.
14. To serve, dip a sharp knife in hot water, dry it off quickly and slice.

SUGGESTED WINE:
Sauterne Château Filhot - Francia

TORTA DELLA DOMENICA
Sunday Cake

Génoise (see recipe on page 79)	3 12″/30 cm discs, ½″/1 cm thick
Pastry cream (see recipe on page 69)	1 qt/1 lt
Unsweetened chocolate	7 oz/200 gr, grated
Milk chocolate	7 oz/200 gr, grated
Heavy (double) cream	1 cup/200 cc

FOR THE SYRUP

Sugar	1 ⅓ cup/250 gr
Boiling water	2 ¼ cups/500 cc
Strega, brandy or your spirit of choice	¼ cup/50 cc
or, for a non-alcaholic cake	
Strong espresso coffee	¼ cup/50 cc

1. Dissolve the sugar in the boiling water. Mix in the spirit of you choice or the coffee.

TO ASSEMBLE THE CAKE

1. Divide the pastry cream in two. Mix into one half, while it's still hot, the grated unsweetened chocolate.
2. Soak the first génoise disc with a third of the syrup.
3. Spread the chocolate pastry cream over the génoise.
4. Place the second génoise disc over the first and soak with the second third of the syrup.
5. Spread the plain pastry cream over the gènoise.
6. Soak the third génoise disc with the remaining syrup then turn it over and place it on the cake.
7. Bring the heavy (double) cream to a boil pour it over the grated milk chocolate in a bowl. Stir until all the chocolate has melted and amalgamated with the cream. Allow to cool.
8. Pour the chocolate evenly over the entire cake, covering it all. Use a spatula to coat the sides.
9. This cake is even more delicious after having been refrigerated overnight.

- As a variation, you can add a few spoons of cherry preserves to the plain pastry cream.

SUGGESTED WINE:
Lacryma Christi del Vesuvio Liquoroso Bianco - Campania
Vernaccia di Serra Petrosa Dolce Rosso - Marche

TORTA DI FICHI
Fig Tart

Shortbread dough (see recipe on page 78)	1 lb/500 gr
Pan di Spagna (see recipe on page 74)	a 12″/30 cm disc
Pastry cream, dense and cold (see recipe on page 69)	1 ½ cups/300 gr
Apricot jam	3 tablespoons
Fresh, firm figs	10
Walnut halves	20
Butter	as needed
Raw sugar	¼ cup/50 gr
Vin Santo	¼ cup/50 cc

1. Grease a 12″/30 cm spring-form cake tin.
2. Line the bottom of the tin with parchment paper.
3. Roll out the shortbread dough and lay it onto the bottom of the cake tin. Trim the dough, then roll out a long strip that will line the sides of the tin.
4. Spread the apricot jam evenly over the base of the tart.
5. Place a pan di spagna disc about ¼″/½ cm thick over the jam.
6. Sprinkle the pan di spagna with the Vin Santo.
7. Spread the pastry cream over the cake.
8. Slice the figs as you see best and arrange them decoratively over the pastry cream.
9. Distribute the walnut halves among the figs.
10. Sprinkle the tart with the raw sugar and bake at 350°F/180°C/Gas Mark 4 for 45 minutes.
11. Allow the tart to rest for a day before serving.
12. When you're ready to serve the tart, remove the springform and slide the tart onto a serving dish.

SUGGESTED WINE:
Moscato Passito Bianco - Molise
Vin Santo - Toscana

TORTA DI FRAGOLINE
Wild Strawberry Tart

Shortbread dough (see recipe on page 78)	1 lb/500 gr
Pan di Spagna (see recipe on page 74)	a 12″/30 cm disc
Pastry cream, dense and cold (see recipe on page 69)	1 ½ cups/300 gr
Wild strawberries	2 ½ cups/500 gr
Apricot jam	2 tablespoons
Dry beans	1 lb/500 gr
Parchment paper	a 12″/30 cm disc

FOR THE SYRUP

Boiling water	⅛ cup/25 cc
Maraschino liqueur	2 tablespoons/25 cc

1. Prepare the shortbread dough according to the recipe. Roll it out and place it in a 12″/30 cm springform cake tin.
2. Pierce the entire bottom of the shortbread with a fork, cover it with the parchment paper and fill the tart shell with the dried beans.
3. Bake at 350°F/180°C/Gas Mark 4 for 20 minutes on the bottom shelf of the oven.
4. Remove from the oven and let cool before removing the beans and paper.
5. Spread the bottom of the tart with most of the apricot jam, then place the pan di spagna disc. Spoon the vin santo syrup over the pan di spagna, uniformly soaking it. This operation can be done very well using a brush rather than a spoon.
6. Spread the cold pastry cream over the pan di spagna.
7. Arrange the strawberries over the cream in concentric circles, in an orderly, decorative manner.
8. Use a brush to cover the strawberries with the rest of the apricot jam which will have been warmed slightly to make it more fluid and easy to spread.

SUGGESTED WINE:
Brachetto d'Acqui Rosso - Piemonte

TORTA GANACHE AL PISTACCHIO
Pistachio Ganache Tart

It was a chilly winter December evening. A group of friends was gathered around the fire-place eating roasted chestnuts, chocolates and sipping a fine Amarone. Our conversation was accompanied by the music of Paolo Conte. Our talk was about the invention of new sweets and cakes - our ideas were surreal.Imagine a chocolate that instead of weighing a quarter of an ounce, weighs four and a half pounds!

Milk chocolate	1 lb/500 gr
Unsweetened chocolate	1 lb/500 gr
Heavy (double) cream	1 cup/250 cc
Confectioners sugar	¾ cup/150 gr
Chopped pistachio	1 cup/200 gr
Whole pistachio	24

1. Prepare the pistachio ganache: Grate the milk chocolate (use a food processor if you have one).
2. Bring the cream to a boil with ½ cup/100 gr of the confectioners' sugar. Add the grated chocolate and cook, stirring, until you obtain a dense cream.
3. Add the chopped pistachios.
4. Meanwhile, melt the grated unsweetened chocolate in a double boiler or bain-marie.
5. Line a 12"/30 cm pizza or pie tin with clear plastic cling wrap.
6. Pour in half of the melted unsweetened chocolate, rotating and turning the tin in order that the entire base and sides are covered.
7. Let cool.
8. When the chocolate has cooled and hardened, pour the ganache over it, sprea-ding it evenly.
9. Arrange the whole pistachios around the circumference, as if they were the mi-nutes on a clock.
10. Refrigerate for 2 hours, then cover the surface with the rest of the other half of the melted unsweetened chocolate. Try to over the ganache evenly.
11. Return to the refrigerator for 2 more hours.
12. Cover the cake with transparent plastic wrap, take it out of the tin and holding it upright on the table, run the palm of your hand around the edges. In doing this, the chocolate will warm slightly - your hand motions will smooth the rough spots.
13. Place the tart on a dish of a smaller diameter and, using a hair blower, warm the surface of the tart. Dust immediately with the cocoa powder which will adhere to the softened chocolate.
14. Place the tart on a serving dish and present under a glass bell.

TORTA "LIBIDINE MOSTRUOSA"
"Montrously Indecent" Tart

Can you imagine a "monstrously indecent" tart? Well, let's make one together!

Unsweetened chocolate	1 lb/500 gr	Confectioners' sugar	¾ cups/200 gr
Robust red wine	1 cup/250 cc	Crushed or chopped	¾ cups/200 gr
Heavy (double) cream	1 cup/250 cc	Whole cocoa beans	24

FOR THE COATING
Unsweetened chocolate	1 ¾ cups/400 gr

1. Grate the chocolate.
2. Bring the cream, wine and sugar to a boil, then stir in half of the grated chocolate. Cook, stirring, until you've obtained a dense cream.
3. Mix in the chopped cocoa beans.
4. In the meantime, prepare the coating: melt the other half of the grated chocolate in a double boiler or bain-marie.
5. Line a 12"/30 cm pizza or cake tin with transparent plastic cling wrap.
6. Pour half of the chocolate covering onto the tin and, turning and rotating the tin, cover the entire surface evenly. The covering should be very thin.
7. When the covering has hardened, pour the ganache with the crushed cocoa beans over it.
8. Arrange the whole cocoa beans around the circumference of the surface of the tart, as if they were the minutes on the face of a clock.
9. Refrigerate for half an hour, then pour the rest of the covering over the tart such that its surface is entirely coated.
10. Return to the refrigerator for at least two hours.
11. Remove the tart from the cake tin. Holding it upright on the work surface, run the palm of your hands along the edges to smooth out any rough spots.
12. Use a blow dryer to briefly warm the surface of the tart before you dust it with cocoa powder. This way, the powder will stick to the tart.!
13. To serve, place the tart on a serving dish and cover with a glass dome.

- Do not refrigerate.
- Slice using a sharp knife dipped in hot water then immediately wiped dry, or break it apart.

SUGGESTED WINE:
Brunesco Fattoria Montagliari - Toscana, Amarone Valpolicella - Veneto

TORTA DI MELE DI ELLY
Elly's Apple Tart

*This recipe is from my cousin, Elly Cioffi, one of the most
intelligent people I have ever known.*

All purpose flower	1 ½ cups/300 gr
Sugar	1 ½ cups/300 gr
Eggs	2
Egg yolks	2
Butter	½ cup/100 gr, melted
Milk	½ cup/100 cc
Bread crumbs	½ cup/100 gr
Granulated yeast	1 packet
Salt	a pinch
The zest of 1 organic lemon	
Apples	2
Confectioners' sugar	½ cup/100 gr

1. Grease a cake tin and sprinkle with bread crumbs.
2. Peel and thinly slice the apples.
3. Toss the sliced apples in the melted butter and mixed in the sugar.
4. Arrange the apple slices in a circular pattern on the base of the cake tin.
5. Mix together the eggs, egg yolks, the rest of the sugar, flour, salt, lemon zest, milk and yeast together.
6. Cover the apple slices with this batter.
7. Bake at 350°F/180°C/Gas Mark 4 for 40 minutes.
8. Remove from the oven and allow to cool before turning it over onto a serving dish.
9. Sprinkle with confectioners' sugar.

SUGGESTED WINE:
Albana di Romagna Amabile DOCG - Emilia Romagna

TORTA MALAKOFF

This recipe was given to me by a childhood friend.

Pan di Spagna (see recipe on page 74)	1 ½ lb / 700 gr
Pastry cream (see recipe on page 69)	2 cups / 500 gr
Mixed fresh fruit	2 cups / 500 gr
(pears, banans, peaches, strawberries)	
Maraschino liqueur	¼ cup / 50 cc
Whipped cream	2 cups / 500 cc

FOR THE SYRUP

Sugar	1 ½ cups / 250 gr
Boiling water	2 cups / 500 cc
Strega, Brandy or any liqueur	¼ cup / 50 cc
of your choice	

- Dissolve the sugar in the boiling water along with the liqueur of your choice

1. Line the inside of a round bowl with transparent plastic wrap.
2. Line the bowl with slices of pan di Spagna that have been soaked in the syrup.
3. Cut the fruit into little pieces and toss with the Maraschino.
4. Mix the fruit with the pastry cream.
5. Put a couple of spoonsful of the fruity cream into the bowl, then cover with slices of pan di spagna. Repeat until you've filled the bowl with layers of cream and, finally, a top layer of pan di Spagna.
6. Soak this top layer with the last of the syrup.
7. Cover with plastic wrap and refrigerate overnight.
8. Before serving, turn the cake upside down onto a serving dish and decorate with the whipped cream.

TRIFLE

Pan di Spagna (see recipe on page 74)	2 discs
Pastry cream (see recipe on page 69)	1 qt/1 lt, not very dense
Peaches in syrup	2 jars, thinly sliced
Raspberry jam	1 jar
Confectioners' sugar	¾ cup/150 gr
Cognac	to taste
Heavy (double) cream	1 ½ cups/300 cc
Fresh raspberries	¾ cup/150 gr

1. Line a 12"/30 cm springform cake tin or a round bowl with transparent plastic wrap.
2. Lay down a disc of pan di Spagna in the springform and generously sprinkle it with cognac.
3. Alternate at least two layers of pastry cream and peaches.
4. Spoon most of the raspberry jam over the cream in dollops.
5. Top with the other pan di Spagna disc, soak with cognac. Cover with plastic wrap and refrigerate overnight.
6. Before serving, turn the trifle upside down onto a serving dish.
7. Warm the remaining jam in a saucepan along with an equal amount of confectioners sugar.
8. Cover the trifle with the raspberry glaze.
9. Decorate with whipped cream and fresh raspberries.

- This version of trifle is served, spooning it into individual cups.

1. To assemble the trifle in a clear glass bowl so that it can be admired in all its temptation!
2. Arrange alternating slices of pan di Spagna soaked with cognac, peach slices and raspberry jam in a bowl until the bowl is almost full.
3. Pour the pastry cream over the trifle. The cream should be rather thin and hot so that it will penetrate the layers of pan di Spagna. In order to facilitate this, poke some holes through the layers using a dull knife or the handle of a fork.
4. Cover the trifle with plastic wrap and refrigerate overnight.
5. Before serving, decorate the top of the trifle with whipped cream and fresh raspberries.

TWANSIES

I created these little treats when I found myself with extra egg whites that were left over from another recipe. Chewy and delicious! A really tempting variation is to mix into the batter little pieces of bittersweet, milk or gianduja chocolate.

Almond or hazlenut flour	1 ½ cups / 300 gr
	(or pine nuts or pistachios)
Chopped almonds (or other nuts)	½ cup / 100 gr
Whole almonds (or other nuts)	¼ cup / 50 gr
The zest of 1 organic lemon	
Sugar	1 cup / 200 gr
Egg whites	4, beaten until stiff

1. Mix the nut flour with the sugar and add as much beaten egg white as is necessary to obtain a rather dense batter.
2. Grease 30-40 small paper baking cups.
3. Place a small amount of chopped nuts in each cup, then cover with a spoonful of batter. Place a whole nut on top of each twansy.
4. Arrange the paper cups on a cookie sheet and bake at 350°F / 180°C / Gas Mark 4 for 10-15 minutes, or until the top has formed a golden crust.
5. Allow to cool and serve in their little paper cups.

SUGGESTED WINE:

Vin Santo invecchiato - Toscana
Passito di Pantelleria - Sicilia

ZEPPOLE DI SAN GIUSEPPE

Zeppole are a southern Italian specialty. Traditional zeppole is are simple fritters prepared with hot water, flour and lard. Saint Joseph's zeppole are a richer version that are made to celebrate the feast of St. Joseph in March.

Boiling water	2 cups/500 cc
All purpose flour	1 ½ cups/350 gr
Sugar	¾ cup/200 gr
Eggs	5
Extra virgin olive oil	1 cup/250 cc
Marsala or other sweet wine	¼ cup/55 cc
Bay leaves	2
Salt	a pinch
Confectioners' sugar	as needed
Dense pastry cream (see recipe on page 69)	1 cup/250 gr
Cherry preserves	as needed

1. Bring the water to a boil in a saucepan along with the bay leaves, sugar, olive oil and salt.
2. When the sugar has completely dissolved, remove the bay leaves and add the flour all at once.
3. Use a wooden spoon to mix the batter until it has become glossy and no longer sticks to the side of the pot.
4. Allow to cool to room temperature.
5. Mix in an egg, stirring until it's been completely absorbed. Continue in this way, one egg at a time until they've all been absorbed by the batter.
6. Add the wine, stirring vigorously.
7. Spoon the batter into a pastry bag with a zig-zag tip and squeeze it out into round "doughnut" shapes without the holes.
8. Fry the zeppole in abundant hot oil.
9. When the zeppole are golden brown, use a slotted spoon to remove them to a dish covered with paper towels to absorb the excess oil.
10. Sprinkle each zeppola with confectioners sugar. Spoon a dollop of pastry cream on each one and onto each dollop of cream, a dot of cherry preserve.

- The zeppole can also be baked in the oven, resulting in a lighter treat. Line a baking sheet with parchment paper. Squeeze the batter out in ring shapes, leaving ample room between them as they will grow in the oven. Bake at 350°F/180°C /Gas Mark 4 for 15 minutes or until golden.

ZUPPA INGLESE

"English soup", is the Italian version of English trifle. It was a very popular and stylish dessert in the 1950's and is still a favorite. What gives zuppa inglese its distinctive color is the "Alchèrmes", a scarlet red liqueur, which can be found in many specialty stores. In absence of Alchèrmes, you can use Maraschino.

FOR THE SYRUP

Water	1 ½ cups / 300 gr
Sugar	1 cups / 200 grams
Cognac	¼ cup 50 cc
Pan di Spagna (see recipe on page 74)	1 ¼ lb / 600 gr
Pastry cream (see recipe on page 69)	2 lb / 1 kg
Chocolate pastry cream (see recipe on page 68)	1 ¼ cup / 250 gr
Cherry preserves	1 jar
Alchèrmes	½ cup / 100 cc
Whipped cream	2 ½ cups / 500 cc
Cocoa powder	as needed

1. Prepare the syrup by dissolving the sugar in the boiling water along with the cognac. When the sugar has completely dissolved, remove from the heat and allow to cool.
2. Cut the pan di Spagna in thick slices which will be soaked with the syrup.
3. Line a glass bowl with the syrup-soaked slices of pan di Spagna. Pour a third of the pastry cream and half of the chocolate pastry cream over the pan di Spagna. Spoon half of the cherry preserves over all and sprinkle with Alchèrmes.
4. Lay down another layer of pan di Spagna soaked with syrup, and cover with half of the remaining pastry cream, the rest of the chocolate cream, the rest of the cherry preserves, and sprinkle with Alchèrmes.
5. Lay down a final layer of pan di Spagna soaked with syrup. Cover with the last of the pastry cream. Decorate, completely covering the zuppa inglese, with the whipped cream.
6. Refrigerate overnight.
7. To serve the zuppa inglese, spoon it into individual dessert cups and decorate with sifted powdered cocoa.

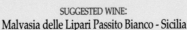

SUGGESTED WINE:
Malvasia delle Lipari Passito Bianco - Sicilia

FIRST PUBLISHED IN ITALY, APRIL, 2013
PRINTED BY TIPOGRAFIA GRAFICA GIORGETTI
VIA DI CERVARA 10
ROME